Gustave De Ridder

A Personal history of the Horse-guards from 1750 to 1872

Gustave De Ridder

A Personal history of the Horse-guards from 1750 to 1872

ISBN/EAN: 9783741143427

Manufactured in Europe, USA, Canada, Australia, Japa

Cover: Foto ©Thomas Meinert / pixelio.de

Manufactured and distributed by brebook publishing software
(www.brebook.com)

Gustave De Ridder

A Personal history of the Horse-guards from 1750 to 1872

A PERSONAL HISTORY

OF

THE HORSE-GUARDS

FROM 1750 TO 1872.

BY

J. H. STOCQUELER,

AUTHOR OF
"THE HISTORY OF THE BRITISH ARMY."
&c., &c.

IN ONE VOLUME.

LONDON:
HURST AND BLACKETT, PUBLISHERS,
13 GREAT MARLBOROUGH STREET.
1873.

CHAPTER XIX.

CHAPTER XX.

CHAPTER XXI.

CHAPTER XXII.

CONTENTS.

CHAPTER I.

CHAPTER II.

CHAPTER I.

THE glory of the dingy old edifice known as "The Horse-Guards" has departed.

The Clock, so long proverbial for its truth to time still indicates with tolerable punctuality the progress of the day; the stalwart troopers of the Life-Guards or "the Blues" still tenant the ugly boxes on either side of the main gate facing Whitehall, exciting the admiration of boys and nurse-maids, and the surprise of sober-minded rustics and intelligent foreigners, who cannot see the sense of such immobility of horse and man, or comprehend the power and self-command through which it is achieved.

But the Clock is no longer the recognised authority by which passers-by erst set their watches, and exulted in the correspondence of opinion between the old-established time-piece and their own diminutive dials. Electricity has destroyed the prestige of the Clock, and transferred public loyalty to the Ball at Charing Cross, which is understood to be in secret collusion with the Greenwich Observatory; while the gigantic dragoons, who proudly kept watch and ward over the persons and the records of the War Minister, the Commander-in-Chief, and all the General and Personal Head-Quarters Staff, have faded into doleful mutes at the portals of the "dear departed." *Sic transit!* The whole affair has become matter of history.

At the time the building familiarly known as "The Horse-Guards" was erected, the Army was not twenty thousand strong. It had been weakened by its employment on the Continent and in the North of England, notably in service against the forces of the Pretender.

In 1752, when a vote was asked for £16,000 to pay the salaries of the General and Staff Officers, there was much opposition in Parliament. From the reports of speeches made by Members

disguised under the names of celebrated Roman
republicans, meeting in the "Political Club,"
it appears that "T. Sempronius Gracchus" (Lord
Perceval) was particularly hostile to the office of
Captain-General, then held by the Duke of
Cumberland. He did not see the use of such
an officer, nor of inferior Generals and Aides-de-
Camp, in a time of peace. Nor was he without
apprehension that the Captain-General might,
like another Cromwell, be too powerful for the
Crown, and employ the Army against the institutions he should defend. He would apparently
have been content to disband the Army, until
a war should render its services necessary.
His reasoning resembled that of the very careful
matron who did not wish her son to go into
the water until he had learnt to swim. He
had a strange faith in impromptu armies
which had never acquired any notion of their
duties.

When it was proposed to fix the force
at 18,857 men, "Horatius Cocles" (Mr. J. Hyde
Cotton), who was opposed to a standing army
moved an amendment reducing it to 15,000.

Mr. Beckford, whose sayings are reported under the pseudonym of "A. Bæculorius," thought England could always get mercenaries from abroad, but Mr. G. Lee, a lawyer ("Livius Salinator"), and others, were in favour of the force (18,800) and the vote passed.

Authorities differ as to the exact date when the first stone of the "Horse-Guards" was laid, but there is no doubt that the edifice must have been completed—all but the dome and the turret—in the year 1750.

At that time, British architects apparently took their tone from the form and stature of the Hanoverian family. Neither George I. nor George II. was cast in the mould on which "every god had set his seal to give the world assurance of a man." They were rather dumpy and stumpy than the reverse, and it was a delicate compliment on the part of the architects and builders to lay on the enduring earth heavy loads of masonry, whose outline and elevation should correspond with the bulk and height of the Monarchs.

At the present day, we should be rather disinclined to assign the epithet "magnificent" to the dismal archway which leads from St. James's Park to Whitehall, but it was so designated on the occasion of George II. passing beneath it in 1751. The dome and steeple of the building were raised at a later period, for within the concave there appears, carved in oak· beneath the Royal crown and monogram, the date 1759.

The original purpose of the building was to constitute a barrack for the two troops of the "Royal Horse-Guards—Blue," which were accommodated on the ground-floor of the right and left wings.

The Guard which mounted there every morning was part of the "King's Guard," which assembled daily in the precincts of the Palace. Its movements were regulated by the "Gold Stick in Waiting," an officer of high rank, and one of the Colonels of the three regiments constituting the Household Cavalry Brigade.

But it is not with the mere masonry of the Horse-Guards that we propose to deal. The edifice derives its importance less from its peculiar architecture (for, as Charles Knight truly

said in his "London," "it is without flattery
the ugliest building in the metropolis"), than
from the work that has been carried on within
its walls.

Hopes and fears have herein agitated the
hearts of thousands of men, whose prospects
in life rested on the decrees of the potentates
who governed, at different periods, the destinies
of the Army. Here, adulation, in search of
preferment, has crooked the pregnant hinges of
the knee,—

"That thrift might follow fawning;"

here, the wronged and neglected have clamoured,
and often clamoured vainly, for justice; here,
valour has received the guerdon it fairly earned,
or intrigue has triumphed over the claims of
merit and long service; here, outside influences
have not unfrequently warped a chief's nobler
impulses; and here, too, incapacity, error, and
impropriety have been visited with stern rebuke
and chastisement.

But, on the whole, with all the defects im-
putable to the Horse-Guards, high honour, strict

integrity, and a sense of true desert have far
more generally characterised the acts and bearing
of the rulers for the time, than those qualities of
despotism, on the one hand, and subserviency
on the other, which often furnished ground of
private remonstrance and public censure.

When the building in Whitehall was first par-
tially used as the offices of the War Department,
the command of the Army was in the hands of
Lord Ligonier.

Ligonier was an officer of rare distinction. He
had served in all the wars in Queen Anne's reign,
under the Duke of Marlborough, and in every
succeeding war, "with a bravery and conduct
that deservedly raised him to the chief posts in
his profession."

His commission as Commander-in-Chief. was
dated in 1757.

His gallantry in the field was the theme of
several of the poetasters' of the time. Their
turgid stuff would not be tolerated at the present
day, but in the Georgian era it seemed to have
been *de rigueur*.

One of those gentlemen, too modest to pro-

claim himself, published an "Ode on Martial
Virtue," in a folio volume, and after dwelling
prosaically on the state of poetry in England,
burst into a rapturous eulogy in verse, of which
Ligonier was the object :—

> "Monuments of endless praise
> Clio raised, and still shall raise
> To the Chiefs of Mighty Name,
> Just inheritors of Fame;
> Thus, by her eternal laws,
> Live her Churchills and Nassaus.
> This gift, O Ligonier! receive,
> A garland which the Musos weave;
> Not of the fading verdure made,
> Which groans in Chiswick's awful shade ;
> But of immortal blessings wove,
> From Pindus and the Aonian Grove."

At the battle of Laufeld, in 1747, Lord (then
Sir John) Ligonier, who commanded the cavalry,
was made prisoner. Taken before Louis XV.,
the King was so well pleased with him, that he
sent Sir John to England on his parole.   Sir
John then received the Order of the Bath, and
was nominated " General of His Majesty's Horse
Forces."   He was subsequently raised to the
Peerage, and created a Field-Marshal.

Lord (then Sir John) Ligonier had also been present at the battle of Fontenoy, where the "bashful Dutch"—the "ungenerous Dutch," as Kane, the military historian, with remarkable forbearance, politely refers to the sluggish allies —holding back at critical moments, Ligonier's Horse (the Fourth) exhibited great "alacrity, conduct, and bravery."

Before the regiment proceeded on foreign service it had been quartered and recruited in Ireland, and in fact was borne on the Irish Establishment from the conclusion of Queen Anne's reign to the year 1742.

On its coming over to England to embark for Germany, it was reviewed by George II., at the same time with the Blues and Lord Pembroke's Horse. After the review the King said to Ligonier :—

"Ligonier, your men have the air of soldiers, but their horses look poorly. How is that ?"

"Sire," replied the Colonel, "the men are *Irish*, and gentlemen ; the horses are *English*."

This terse reply was of a piece with the epigrammatic retort of Sir A. Agnew. The King

remarked to him on the day of the battle of
Dettingen,—

"Sir Andrew, the *gens d'armes* got in among
you to-day."

"Yes, your Majesty," quietly made answer
Sir Andrew, "but they did not get out
again."

It does not appear that, one hundred and
twenty years ago, "the Horse-Guards" was the
head-quarters of the Commander-in-Chief, for all
Lord Ligonier's orders were dated from " Knights-
bridge Barracks." The Secretary for War, however, issued Orders and Warrants from the
Horse-Guards, and seemed indeed to perform a
large part of those functions which, at a later
period, were transferred to the Commander-in-
Chief.

There are not many of those documents, now
called Circular Memoranda (of the time), extant,
but one of them published in 1759, shows that,
even at that period, the Purchase system was a
subject of vexation to the Government.

Notice was given from the War Office (Horse-
Guards) that whoever intended to purchase a

commission, was first to inform himself whether the commission for which he was in treaty might be sold, with the King's leave, and, "in all instances, where it shall be found that any money or other considerations have been given for a commission, not openly sold with the leave of His Majesty, the person obtaining such commission shall be superseded."

The year 1762 inaugurated a long peace. The treaty of Fontainebleau was signed, putting an end to the Seven Years' War. The troops that had been employed in Germany returned home, and gave themselves up to the loose pleasures incidental to a life of inaction.

The Command-in-Chief of the Army abroad was at this time in the hands of the Duke of Cumberland, who had distinguished himself by his generalship (somewhat tarnished by an alleged cruelty at the battle of Culloden, in 1745) but more by his personal bravery at the battle of Dettingen, where he was wounded. The wound broke out again in 1764, although inflicted in 1743, when the Duke was twenty-two years of age. He died of mortification and inflammation arising from the renewal of the injury, in the forty-fourth year of his age.

Ligonier appears to have got out of the good graces of the King soon after this, and was superseded by the Marquis of Granby (1766).

CHAPTER II.

CHAPTER II.

THE tone of fulsome panegyric which characterised nearly all the public writers of the
Georgian era, until the eighteenth century was
nearly seventy years old, renders it very difficult
to trace any reliable facts respecting the actual
condition of the British Army.

In 1769 truth finds utterance, for we come to
the memorable epoch when "Junius" startled
society by the boldness and severity of his
strictures. No channel existed in those times
for the complaints of the soldiery, unless they
were published anonymously; the officer who
murmured at his position became a 'marked
man.' But "Junius" opened the eyes of the

public to the state of the Army, which (he wrote
on January 21, 1769,) was "moulding away for
want of the direction of a man of common
abilities and spirit." The Marquis of Granby
was then Commander-in-Chief. Of him "Junius"
wrote :—

"It has lately been a fashion to pay a compliment to the bravery and generosity of the Commander-in-Chief at the expense of his under-
standing. They who love him make no question
of his courage, while his friends dwell chiefly on
the facility of his disposition.

"Admitting him to be as brave as a total
absence of all feeling and reflection can make
him, let us see what sort of merit he derives from
the remainder of his character. If it be generosity
to accumulate in his own person and family a
number of lucrative employments; to provide at
the public expense for every creature that bears
the name of Manners ; and, neglecting the merits
and services of the rest of the Army, to heap
promotions upon his favourites and dependants,
the present Commander-in-Chief is the most
generous man alive.

"Nature has been sparing of her gifts to the noble lord; but where birth and fortune are united, we expect the noble pride and independence of a man of spirit, not the servile, humiliating complaisance of a courtier.

"As to the goodness of his heart, if a proof of it be taken from the facility of never refusing, what conclusion shall we draw from the decency of never performing? And if the discipline of the Army be in any way preserved, what thanks are due to a man whose cares, notoriously confined to filling up vacancies, have degraded the office of Commander-in-Chief into a broker of commissions?"

The Marquis would probably have escaped with this single notice from the troublesome "*nominis umbra*," had not Colonel Sir W. Draper, in the exuberance of his solicitude for the honour of Lord Granby, justified the prayer for salvation from "our friends" by dwelling upon his virtues and disinterestedness.

"His courage," quoth Draper, in replying to "Junius," "though of the brightest and most ardent kind, is among the lowest of his numerous

c 2

good qualities. He was formed to excel in war by Nature's liberality to his mind, as well as person.

"Educated and instructed by his most noble father, and a most spirited as well as excellent scholar, the Bishop of Bangor, he was trained to the nicest sense of honour and to the truest and noblest sort of pride, that of never doing or suffering a mean action.

"A sincere love and attachment to his King and country, and to their glory, first impelled him to the field, where he never gained aught but honour. He impaired through his bounty his own fortune, for his bounty was founded upon the noblest of human affections; it flows from a heart melting to goodness from the most refined humanity."

Just as Sir W. Draper's panegyric appears to have been, according to concurrent testimony, it enabled the irrepressible "Junius" to ask whether the "Blues," of which Lord Granby was made Colonel, and the Master-Generalship of the Ordnance, were 'nothing?'

There are no records, either public or private,

of the manner in which the Marquis fulfilled his
duties at the "Horse-Guards," but his popularity
in the Army, acquired during his gallant and
disinterested command of the British forces in
Germany, and his bravery at the battle of
Minden, where he atoned by his activity and
intrepidity for the unaccountable sluggishness of
Lord George Sackville, underwent no decline.

To the last his name was venerated alike by
friend and foe. In the "Biographie Universelle"
we find him described as "Un bon militaire,
brave, actif, généreux, très-aimé des soldats,
dont il s'occupait beaucoup."

The Marquis of Granby died on October 18,
A.D. 1770, " to the irreparable loss of his country
and the inexpressible grief of all true Englishmen." Lord Granby's death was preceded by
that of Lord Ligonier in the same year.

It does not appear that either the Duke of
Cumberland, Lord Ligonier, or the Marquis of
Granby exerted himself much to improve the
condition of the men and officers during the
tenure of their respective commands.

There were two obstacles to the success of

any efforts they might have felt disposed to
employ. The Army had become a mere political
machine for the furtherance of the ends of
Ministers, or a plaything for the King, George
III. His Majesty had studied the art military
as far as 'the bookish theorie' went, and liked
to see his Guards in their ponderous habiliments
and their unwieldy weapons and accoutrements
on parade in the Parks, where he reviewed them
after a fashion.

But here his interest in their welfare stopped.
To behold a line of red-coated infantry and blue-
coated cavalry as clean as pipe-clay, powder,
and pomatum, brick-dust, blacking, and brushes
could make them, was the acme of royal delight:
how these martial results were achieved, His
Majesty left to the Staff and the Secretary at War.
And these gentlemen troubled themselves but
little on the subject.

The King gave away the Colonelcies and
foreign commands to his favourites; the Secretary
of State distributed his share of the patronage
among political adherents. The Army was a
mere vehicle for corruption, and of course,

under such a system, it was going rapidly to destruction.

There was no independent Press in those days, to open the eyes of the country to the probable consequences of official jobbery, royal favouritism, and professional neglect. The Attorney-General would have visited with an *ex-officio* criminal information any printer who should have reflected on the flagrant proceedings of the authorities.

Yet there were not wanting able writers who, under the shelter of a pseudonym, ventured to speak their sentiments in language eloquent and convincing. One of these reviewed the state of the Army in 1779, in an exhaustive work which he modestly called " The Honest Sentiments of an English Officer."

In his view, the depraved condition to which the Army had sunk was attributable entirely to the absence of a Commander-in-Chief, who should be independent of all other official authority and influence. There were officers *nominally* at the head of the force, but in reality and in practice the King himself was Commander-in-Chief.

Against this the "English Officer" protested
emphatically in a lengthened passage worthy of
quotation.

"The first security of the Army's fidelity
to the laws, and its utility to the country,
resides in those to whose command it is entrusted. If burlesque was to employ its active
fancy in inventing the most preposterous ab-
surdity in government, it could hardly pitch
upon a greater than *an army without a chief;*
nor could the sneaking cunning of hypocritical
despotism devise a system more incurably poi-
sonous to a free state.

"In England the King is supreme over all
the forces of the Empire by sea and land;
his conduct is liable to no legal scrutiny; on
the contrary, he is pre-acquitted of every imputation of evil design or error, and his person
is sacred, for *he can do no wrong.* This perfect
union of authority, this independence, and those
attributes, not only give lustre to the Crown,
but guard it, as well as the liberty of the
subject, from those assassinations, civil wars,
anarchies, and tyrannies under which the

Roman Empire and freedom were tortured and
fell.

"Yet, if we were to consider the position
abstractedly by that principle in a limited
monarchy by which the monarch cannot be
punished for his acts, our constitution, instead
of attracting the veneration of the sage, would
be the object of his contemptuous pity, or
his ridicule. But on a further examination
we shall find it provided that the King cannot execute any act of importance without his
Council, and that they are responsible in their
persons and properties to the country for the
advice they give him. . . . . He may
remove from his councils those who refuse
to obey his absolute commands, but then
he must appoint others, for the moment
he passes that boundary he sets his crown on
a *die*.

"The Army, according to its present constitution, is the only department in which no
intermediate person is directly responsible for
its conduct. Analogous, then, to the solid
principles of the constitution to secure the

persons of our present and future Kings sacred
and inviolable, as well as a national control
whose operation over the Army may not exist
in theory only, the office of Commander-in-
Chief must be annually voted with the Army
as a *sine quâ non*, the persons entrusted with
this office to be appointed and removed at
the pleasure of the Crown; but every order
to the Army to pass through their hands,
and every department relative to it to be
subordinate to them.

"This is not to be in *general* what is called
a *Cabinet* employment, that is, not to be
concerned in the little intrigues, corruptions,
and Parliamentary manœuvres incidental to the
usual mode of our administration of parties
or cabals; on the contrary, its very institution is founded to preserve the Army quite
chaste from such prostitution, wherefore this
office, which hath very seldom lain dormant,
but usually subsisted with divided and dis-
putable authority, and consequently very doubt-
ful responsibility, should now be accurately
and positively ascertained in both."

It will scarcely be credited in the face of this extract that, during the period of ten years out of the sixteen which followed upon the death of the Duke of Cumberland, there had been an officer of high rank acting as Commander-in-Chief of the Army.

"Not to speak it profanely," Lord Amherst, the officer in question, seemed to regard his position as little more than a sinecure, or as a Court office to cover the acts of higher powers.

Lord Amherst was a special favourite of the King. He had done some service in America during the war with France, and, as a recompense, on his return home in 1762, was made Governor of Virginia.

In 1768 a misunderstanding arose between Lord Amherst and his royal master, but they were reconciled a few months later, and in 1770 Lord Amherst was appointed Governor of Guernsey.

In 1772 he received the appointment of Lieutenant-General of the Ordnance, and from that time, until 1782, he was Chief of the Staff,

" with three Aides-de-Camp, and to obey such
orders as he shall receive from His Majesty
the Commander-in-Chief;" but he does not
appear to have had the power, if he had the
intention, to improve the condition of the Army
in the slightest degree. In fact, he was
little else than the convenient tool of the
Government. He was held out to the country
as the officer responsible for the condition of
the force, but the strings were pulled by
the Sovereign and the Minister.*

Under such a system the Army degenerated
into a mere rabble, and was easily beaten by
the Americans. Cornwallis, the Howes, Bur-
goyne, and Clinton, with their untutored

* The King "constituted and appointed," so ran the Order,
every one in the Service, down to the Ensigns. Officers in
Parliament who opposed the Ministers were summarily dismissed
the Army. Commissions were assigned to boys at school, and
even children in arms, to ensure them Army seniority; and
when they were old enough to march they were gazetted to regiments, and became captains and field-officers while yet in their
teens. The Duke of Bolton, Lord Westmoreland, Lord Lothian,
Colonel A'Court, and Lord Cobham were among the officers
displaced and disgraced for their political opinions.

officers, and their men drawn from the lowest grades of society, were no match for Washington, Putnam, Schuyler, and their earnest followers.

CHAPTER III.

CHAPTER III.

UPON the break-up of Lord North's Administration in 1782, the Marquis of Rockingham
formed a Government, and General Conway was
appointed Commander-in-Chief, in supersession
of Amherst.

Conway entered the Army as Captain-Lieutenant of the Guards in 1741. Five years later
he was appointed aide-de-camp to the Duke
of Cumberland. During the war in Germany
he was second in command under the Marquis
of Granby, and was much commended for the
talent and courage he displayed.

But he was better known and respected as
a fearless politician than a successful commander.
He had been a Secretary of State under the

previous Government of Lord Rockingham in 1765, and at one time held the Court office of Groom of the Bedchamber, losing the office through his objectionable political opinions.

Whiggism was at a discount in the reign of George III., and Conway was a very decided Whig. The Duke of Devonshire, who regarded him as a martyr to his political opinions, bequeathed him £5,000 as a mark of esteem and veneration for his virtue and integrity, and a compensation for the loss his virtue had entailed upon him.

It was Conway who brought in a Bill for the repeal of the American Stamp Act, which, if carried at the time, might have averted the War of Independence, which cost England so much in blood, treasure, and prestige, without an equivalent.

Edmund Burke, speaking of General Conway's exertions on that memorable occasion, said in the House of Commons (April 1774) :—

" I remember, with a melancholy pleasure, the situation of the Honourable General who made the motion for the repeal, in the crisis when the whole trading interest of this Empire crammed into your lobbies with a trembling expectation; waited, almost to a winter's return of light, their fate from your resolution.

"When at length you had determined in their favour, and your doors thrown open showed them the figure of their deliverer in the well-earned triumph of his important victory, from the whole of the grave multitude there arose an involuntary burst of gratitude and transport. They jumped upon him like children on a long-absent father. They clung about him as captives about their deliverer.

"All England, all America joined in his applause, nor did he seem insensible to the best of all earthly rewards, the love and admiration of his fellow-citizens. Hope elevated and joy brightened his crest. I stood near him, and his face, to use the expression of the Scripture of the first martyr, 'his face was as if it had been the face of an angel.' I do not know how others feel, but if I had stood in that situation, I never would have exchanged it for all that kings in their profusion could bestow."

Conway's political career had now in a measure come to an end, and had merged into a superior phase of military life. His appointment as Commander-in-Chief of the Army was hailed with delight in all circles, and regarded as the inauguration of a reform in the composition of the forces.

Of Lord Amherst, his immediate predecessor in the command, mention has already been made. Horace Walpole spoke of him very contemptuously in one of his letters to Mr. Horace Mann.

A crisis had arrived in the fortunes of the country. The combined fleets of France and Spain were at the mouth of the Channel; Lord Howe, though with an inferior force was watching them, and was described as a very different sea-captain from "such old women as Hardy or Derby," and had a most chosen set of officers, men, and ships.

"As at land," wrote Walpole, "we have General Conway, instead of *that log of wood Lord Amherst*, whose *stupidity and incapacity are past belief*, though, before he was known, he was for a moment a hero,—for one moment supposed a great man, *the Lord knows why.*"

Writing to another party on the same subject, Horace Walpole says :—

" Another advantage we have is in Mr. Conway's being at the head of the Army. With him nobody stands in competition. His military knowledge is unquestionably without a rival. His predecessor, Lord Amherst, was as much below all rivals. There is no word for him but downright stupidity. Had 5,000 French landed while he commanded, he would have been found totally incapable of pressing or putting in motion the least opposition. I could tell you facts that would not be believed, though known to every ensign in the Army."

After Walpole became Lord Orford he suffered his love for, and admiration of, General Conway to betray him into the courtship of the Muses.

In Miss Berry's " Journals and Correspondence " the following effusion appears, headed, " Lines to General Conway :"—

" When Fontenoy's impurpled plain
  Shall vanish from th' historic page,
  Thy youthful valour shall in vain
  Have taught the Gaul to shun thy rage.

" When hostile squadrons round thee stood
  On Laffelts' unsuccessful field,
  Thy captive sabre, drenched in blood,
  The vaunting victor's triumph sealed.

" Forget we these! Let Scotland, too,
  Culloden from her annals tear,
  Lest Envy and her factious crew
  Should sigh to meet thy laurels there."

That will do : there are more stanzas, but
it is impossible not to agree with Lord Orford
himself who displays a sound critical judgment,
in calling them "sad stuff." He intimates in
his letter to Miss Berry that " they were literally
conceived and executed between Hammersmith
and Hyde Park Corner."

The reader will be reminded, by this avowal,
of the rapid act of composition ascribed to
" Sir Benjamin Backbite" by his uncle "Crab-
tree." " Sure never were seen two such beautiful ponies," &c., was a composition "done in

a crack, and on horseback too!" The "art of easy writing what should be easy reading" is given to few persons, and Lord Orford, poetically considered, was certainly not among the number.

The Whigs did not remain in office more than two years. Lord Rockingham's Administration broke up in 1783, and as the vicious arrangement then existed of considering the Command-in-Chief of the Army a Cabinet appointment, General Conway went out of office with his friends. He retired at once into private life.

Walpole wrote to him :—

"Nobody has any claim on you; you have satisfied every point of honour; you have no cause for being particularly grateful to the Opposition, and you want no excuse for living for yourself. . . . To say the truth, I believe that if you had continued at the head of the Army, you would have ruined yourself."

This last remark referred to General Conway's ready generosity. He was hospitable and benevolent. No officer in pecuniary trouble appealed

to him in vain. His liberality was as conspicuous
as his political independence.

Walpole never seems to have wearied of
panegyrising his friend :—

"His virtues as a man, a husband, a father,
a subject, a senator, are unquestionable. His
disinterestedness is conspicuous—his modesty
most amiable—his attention to his profession
laborious—his courage undaunted."

No one was formally nominated to the command of the Army on the formation of the new
Ministry. The appointment was held in abey-
ance, but it was understood that the King was
the absolute Commander.

In 1783 some orders were issued in respect
to the sale and purchase of commissions and
exchanges, and they were signed by the "Commander-in-Chief" without naming him. The
generality of Ordinances, however, have the
signature of General Fawcett, the Adjutant-
General.

In the meanwhile, the King heaped honours on
Lord Amherst. He gave him the Colonelcy of
the "Second Troop of Horse-Guards," and in

1788 created him a Baron of Great Britain, with
remainder to his nephew, Mr. William Pitt. He
was restored to the appointment of *Acting* Commander-in-Chief, and held it, if any inference is
to be drawn from the observations of his con-
temporaries, rather than his own acts as the
" friend of the soldier," until 1793.

We find Horace Walpole writing in 1791 :—

" I have been to *White Pussy's*," the sobriquet
of Lady Amherst, "this evening. I did not
think her lord, *the Commander-in-Chief*, looked
as if *he* would drive Prince Potemkin out of
Bulgaria."

The real truth was that Lord Amherst was an
easy, good sort of man, who hated trouble, and
was content to let the Secretary at War and the
Adjutant-General manage affairs at the Horse-
Guards in their own way.

In 1786, General Fawcett, the Adjutant-General,
drew up, by *the King's* command, some General
Regulations for the Army, as "a foundation for
establishing among the troops that uniformity
and system in the performance of all Exercises
and Movements which are essentially requisite

for Military operations;" and in 1792, the same
officer published new Regulations for the manual
and platoon, which were adopted.

Mr. Windham, as Secretary at War, in 1794
issued a circular consolidating the allowances
of soldiers, viz., bread money, grass money,
poundage money, and an allowance for necessaries, with a view of putting a stop to the com-
plication of accounts.

Finding that the system of centralisation did
not work well, the King commanded the re-
establishment of the Horse-Guards' Staff in 1793,
and Lord Amherst was formally installed as
Commander-in-Chief. But age and the fatigues
of American service had begun to tell upon the
old soldier, and he was not sorry to be relieved
of his trust in 1795.

He was offered an Earldom on his retirement,
but he preferred the bâton of a Field-Marshal.

Two years later Lord Amherst was gathered
to his fathers. He was eighty-one years of age
when he died in 1797.

His biographers bestowed upon him an honourable epitaph. "He was," said a writer in the

Gentleman's Magazine, " a firm disciplinarian,
but over the soldier's friend; a man of strict
economy, and of a collected and temperate mind,
and ready at all times to hear and redress the
complaints of the Army in general."

It was probably as true then as it ever was,
and still is, that the "evil which men do lives
after them; the good is oft interred with their
bones," but Court politeness forbade the utterance of truth in an epitaph. The admitted fact
of the Army being in a miserable plight in 1795
proves that Lord Amherst's friendship was merely
nominal. His biographer was a civilian, who
could have had no opportunity of judging of the
real necessities of the soldiery.

Sir Herbert Taylor, who became Military
Secretary to the Duke of York, and subsequently
Adjutant-General of the Army, having occasion
before a Military Committee some forty years later
to allude to Lord Amherst, spoke rather favour-
ably of the Commander-in-Chief individually,
while he referred in terms of severe reprehension
to the state of affairs.

" I joined the Army abroad," said Sir Herbert,

"in 1793, and I saw what was the condition of
the Army. Nothing could be more disgraceful;
we were the objects of ridicule to every other
service. Lord Amherst was an officer of considerable experience, and much looked up to. I
think the evil arose very much from the want of
system, and from things having been suffered to
go into decay in every respect."

CHAPTER IV.

THE DUKE OF YORK—MILITARY PATRONAGE—MEASURES FOR
THE IMPROVEMENT OF THE ARMY—SUCCESSES IN INDIA—
EXPECTED INVASION—THE PRINCE OF WALES—HIS PATRIO-
TIC ZEAL AND MILITARY ARDOUR—APPLICATIONS FOR
PROMOTION—REPLY OF THE DUKE OF YORK—CHANGE OF
TACTICS.

CHAPTER IV.

THE confidence which George III. cherished in the integrity and ability of the Duke of York, his second son, now led him to confer upon His Royal Highness the command of the Army.

The Duke of York had not been fortunate in achieving victories over the French; and it would have been surprising if he had, looking at the material with which he was condemned to work, and the character and capability of his foreign allies. But in spite of many disadvantages His Royal Highness had displayed good soldiership, care, caution, and courage, and had earned the good opinion and regard of all who had served under him and his coadjutors in the field.

The Horse-Guards now became the focus
whence radiated all the measures which tended to
convert the Army from a heterogeneous mass of
rough and discordant materials into a solid,
stern, and efficient body of disciplined troops.

The Duke of York had been trained to the
profession of arms. He had seen service. His
sympathies were military. His eyes were open
to the terrible deficiencies of the Army.

It was difficult to get the Minister of the day
to relinquish his hold upon the patronage in
commissions and Staff appointments, but the
rank of the Duke of York, and his declared determination to discharge the trust which the King
had placed in his hands with integrity and disinterestedness and to the advantage of the service, checked, in some degree, the abuses which
sprang out of alleged political exigency.

The Duke's progress was at first unavoidably
slow and cautious, and it was long impeded by
the extent of the mischief which had prevailed,
and by the urgent and unceasing calls for the
means of carrying on military operations in
various parts of the globe, and of providing for

the security of the country against foreign aggression.

The expeditions against the French West India Colonies, and particularly against St. Domingo, proved indeed the grave of a large portion of the best of the British infantry and of the foreign corps, the greater part of whom were soon afterwards reduced.

The embodied Militia, the raising of Fencible corps, the formation of the Volunteer corps, were all *accessories* demanding attention. The great object, however, was to relieve the service of the numerous levies which had been hastily, carelessly, and improvidently undertaken.

One of the first acts of the Duke of York was to weed the Horse-Guards' List of the juveniles who, but for his intervention, would have worn the epaulettes intended for older men; his next to simplify the costume, and rid the soldiery of the powder, pomatum, long tails, and cumbrous appointments which impeded their action and crippled their miserable resources.

Taking a lesson from the soldiers of the

E

French Republic, His Royal Highness discarded
the prim uniforms and habits introduced by
the starch Frederick the Great, and gave
greater freedom to the British troops.

But this was not all. He caused a Code of
Regulations to be drawn up and promulgated,
and countenanced the publication and adoption
of a volume of Instructions for the better performance of Field Exercises and Evolutions.

Kind, courteous, and frank to all who ap-
proached him, the Duke of York infused an
excellent feeling into the British Army, and
by the time he had been ten years at
the Horse-Guards, the force was in so
efficient a condition that no anxiety was
felt by the country, or its Chief, as
to its future success in the field, albeit
the mighty genius of Napoleon Bonaparte was
now diverted to the political subjugation of
England.

From the days of Marlborough to the close
of the eighteenth century, with the exception
of the capture of Quebec and some successes
in India, very few victories had been placed

to the credit of the British arms in land operations; but now between 1800 and 1806, a crop of triumphs distinguished a new *régime.* Seringapatam, Assaye, Deeg and Delhi, Egypt and Maida, Trinidad, Minorca, the Cape of Good Hope and Monte Video, attested the valour, discipline, and efficiency of the troops.

One of the most delicate and difficult duties that could possibly devolve on the Duke of York as Commander-in-Chief, arose out of the expected invasion of a French force in the year 1803.

The Prince of Wales, who was at all times "all for the Land service," and who held the Colonelcy of the 10th Hussars, was smitten with patriotic zeal and military ardour, and conceived that while an enemy threatened the shores of England, his proper place would be at the head of a Division. He had accordingly applied to the King for promotion, but His Majesty was deaf to his entreaties.

When the King gave him the Colonelcy in 1793, he distinctly intimated his objections

to the Heir Apparent's considering the Army
a profession or seeking promotion in the Service. The Prince, however, eight years later,
conceived it his duty on various grounds to
repeat his former application. The circumstances of the time, his military studies, a
desire to emulate the " splendid achievements "
of his predecessors, the obligations imposed
upon him by his birth, the duty of appearing
foremost in contributing to the preservation
of the country; the fear of sinking in the
estimation of the Army; the expectations of
the people of England—the degradation he
felt in seeing all his younger brothers promoted to the rank of General while he remained
a Colonel of Dragoons—all these formed pressing motives for a renewal of the Prince of
Wales' desire for promotion.

He wrote to Mr. Secretary Addington. Mr.
Addington laid his application before the King.
The King applauded the Prince's feelings, and
caused him to be referred to the former decisions of His Majesty. " The King's opinion
being fixed, he desired that no further

motion should be made to him on the subject."

Nothing daunted, the Prince wrote direct to his Royal father. The King sent him an autograph reply, obstinately adhering to his original resolve, adding.

"Should the implacable enemy so far succeed as to land, you will have an opportunity of showing your zeal at the head of your regiment."

The Prince returned to the attack, recalling to the King's recollection an expression used by him in 1798:

"If anything was to arise at home"—the Prince had asked to be sent on foreign service—"you ought to be first and foremost."

No reply was vouchsafed to this letter.

Six weeks elapsed, an extensive promotion in the Army was gazetted, but the Prince's pretensions were not noticed.

He now wrote to his brother, the Duke of York, as Commander-in-Chief, entreating him to lay his application for advancement before the King. The Duke reminded him of the impossibility of his opposing the King's commands, and referred to the former correspondence in 1798.

Three more letters from the Prince reiterated his appeal, to each of which the Duke, with admirable tact, courtesy, and good feeling, returned replies, firmly adhering to his purpose of obeying the King's commands.

The Prince now changed his tactics, and professed not to seek military promotion, but a post in the State correspondent to his rank. Hereupon, the Duke of York adroitly shook off all official responsibility, and wrote:

"This I conceive to be purely a political consideration, and as such totally out of my department; and as I have most carefully avoided at all times and under any circumstances ever interfering on any political points, I must hope that you will not call upon me to deviate from the principles by which I have been invariably governed."

Protesting against the Duke's construction of his language, the Prince discontinued writing,

except to inform Mr. Secretary Addington, at
a later date, of his readiness to join his
regiment, if he should apprehend a visit from
the French.

CHAPTER V.

PREPARATIONS FOR RESISTANCE TO INVASION—AMATEUR
LEVIES—PARLIAMENTARY INFLUENCE—HOSTILE PAMPHLETS
—SELF-WILL OF THE KING—THE LORD-LIEUTENANT OF
IRELAND—PETTICOAT INFLUENCE—MAJOR HOGAN'S PAM-
PHLET—INQUIRY INTO THE CONDUCT OF THE DUKE OF
YORK—MR. BURTON.

CHAPTER V.

THE activity and anxiety of the Duke of York increased while the French Army lay encamped at Boulogne, and every hour augmented the belief in the intended descent of the enemy. To concentrate troops on the Kentish coast, to prepare them for a vigorous resistance by continual drills and frequent appeals to their valour and patriotism, demanded incessant exertion.

An immense body of people had enrolled themselves as Volunteers. Fencible regiments were formed, and the Militia were called out, and all of these were placed under the Duke of York's command, in order to ensure harmony of action.

Neither the Duke, however, nor the Generals
of Brigades and Divisions under his orders, had
much faith in the amateur levies. Sir John
Moore bluntly told Mr. Pitt, the Prime Minister,
who was Lord Warden of the Cinque Ports, that
the place for his corps would be on the hills,
"where they would have a good view of the
battle that might be fought on the shore."

Happily the defeat of the French fleet destined
to convey the invading force extinguished Napoleon's hopes, and the hostile attempt was post-
poned *sine die.*

Notwithstanding the untiring efforts of the
Commander-in-Chief to conduct military details
in such a manner as to ensure the confidence of
all who were placed under his control, the demon
of Parliamentary influence still interfered to
check the current of equitable promotion. And
there was another description of power at work,
which, acting upon the susceptible organisation
of the Duke of York, and availing itself of
occasional *lâches*, arising out of the attractions
of Court pleasures and the dissipations of the
gaming-table, corrupted in some degree the

stream of honourable advancement, and brought
scandal upon the management at the Horse-
Guards.

Numerous pamphlets, descriptive of private
grievances and derelictions from public duty,
appeared in the year 1807. The main burthen
of the complaints was the pernicious interference
of political interests.

"To talk of female influence," wrote an
anonymous writer, "is a fallacious reasoning,
for the instances are very few indeed of preferment being obtained by such means, compared
to the omnipotence of Parliamentary interest.
Thence originates the shameful practice of
thrusting boys into a company over the heads
of all the Lieutenants and Ensigns of the
regiments.

" The Duke has done all that man can do to
check it, but he will never remove the Colossus
of Parliamentary interest—an interest that dis-
dains solicitation but imperiously *demands* from
the hands of the Minister that which no Minister
ever found it convenient to deny. To this
species of influence the Commander-in-Chief

must give way, for it is a species of influence capable of removing both Commander-in-Chief and Minister."

If the Duke of York was obliged sometimes to yield to the desires of Members of Parliament who supported the Government, the King was not always disposed to sanction the interference of the First Lord of the Treasury or the Secretary at War.

Upon one occasion a Captain-Lieutenant Paterson, of a Dragoon regiment, who had been eighteen years in that rank, continually passed over by young men with more money and friends in Parliament, appealed to the King to interfere in his behalf. The good-natured monarch promised he should have the first vacancy, but when it occurred, the Secretary at War told his Majesty the troop had been promised to Lord ——, upon which, said the "brief chronicle" of the day, the King flew into a passion, and exclaimed, "*The Lord above shall not have it!*—make out the commission instantly for Paterson." And it was made out accordingly.

This was not the only instance in which

George III. exhibited a strong self-will in the
matter of military appointments. It had been
usual to allow the Lord-Lieutenant of Ireland
to nominate the successor to any vacant Lieu-
tenant-Colonelcy occurring in that country, but
when (in 1788) the Marquis of Buckingham, the
Lord-Lieutenant, wished to appoint his nephew
Colonel Nugent, to a vacancy, the King, without communicating his intentions or waiting to
go through any official forms, appointed a
Colonel Gwynno.

The Marquis was irate, and wrote bitterly to
his brother, Mr. Grenville, and Mr. Pitt, the Prime
Minister. They could only offer him a few
words of consolation of the " never mind " order.
They knew well enough that it would have been
absurd to have attempted to move so obstinate
a personage as George III. from his determination.

Another case was made public about the same
time, which tended to confirm the rumours in
circulation touching the exercise of petticoat
influence. A Brevet Major Hogan, after waiting
three years for a " noted " promotion, and

seeing eighty majors appointed, forty of whom were his juniors, sold out in disgust, being allowed to receive £1,100, the regulation price of his commission ; but the War Department kept back £400, on the ground that that sum had never been entered on the records of the office.

Hogan threatened to publish all the facts of his case, and ultimately did so. On the day, however, of the publication of an advertisement announcing his intention, a lady called in her carriage at the office of the newspaper in which the advertisement appeared, and obtaining his address, proceeded to Frisk's Hotel, in Brook Street, Bond Street, and sent up a letter by a waiter. The lady was described as possessing a fashionable exterior, and her barouche was attended by two servants in livery.

The letter ran thus :—

" Sir,—The enclosed will answer for the deficit of which you complain, and which was not allowed you through mere oversight. I hope this will prevent the publication of your

intended pamphlet, and if it does, you may rely
on a better situation than the one you had.
When I find that you have given up all idea of
opening your secrets to public view, which would
hurt you with all the Royal Family, I shall make
myself known to you, and shall be happy in
your future acquaintance and friendship, by
which I promise you you will reap much benefit.
If you will recall the advertisement, you shall
hear from me, and your claims shall be re-
warded as they deserve."

Enclosed in this letter were bank-notes for
£400.

Four other officers happening to be at the
hotel at the time of Hogan's receipt of the communication, they signed a certificate of the
authenticity of the offer, and the waiter testified
to the appearance of the lady who had called
with the packet. Hogan would not touch the
money, but advertised that it would be returned to the sender, on application to a person named, at No. 14, Angel Court, Throgmor-
ton Street.

The publication of Major Hogan's pamphlet furnished abundance of gossip in Military circles, and even among the public at large. *Ex fumo dare lucem.*

Keen on the scent, the enemies of the Duke of York—for every man who did not get what he wanted naturally became hostile to His Royal Highness—sought eagerly for other cases of mischievous female interference,[*] and were at length gratified by the introduction in the House of Commons of a motion by a Welsh Colonel, Gwyllm Lloyd Wardle, for an inquiry into the conduct of the Duke of York, in permitting a woman named Mary Anne Clarke, who for six years previously had been living under his protection, to use her influence over him in the disposal of Army commissions, for which she received various sums of money.

The case excited an immense amount of public interest. The House of Commons as-

---

[*] When any great crime was reported to Fouché, the First Napoleon's Police Minister, he invariably exclaimed "*Cherchez la femme*" ("Look for the woman"), believing that a petticoat was at the bottom of every foul scheme. *Verb. sat.*

sented to the inquiry, and it was proved beyond all question that the woman, Clarke, had indulged in the illegal traffic to a considerable extent.

It was by no means clear, however, that the Duke of York was cognizant of these nefarious transactions, and had there remained any doubt upon the subject, His Royal Highness's emphatic declaration on his word of honour must have set the subject at rest. However, the Duke resigned the command of the Army as soon as the vote of the House of Commons had, by a majority of 84, affirmed his innocence. He would not do so while the inquiry was pending, lest it should have been supposed that he entertained any apprehension of an unfavourable result.

Among the defenders of the Duke of York on the occasion of the inquiry, perhaps there was not one more able and disinterested than Mr. Burton, the blind M.P. for Oxford. He was a man who had greatly distinguished himself at the Bar, and was raised to a judgeship, and

performed his duties very efficiently in spite
of his personal misfortune.

He had been ten years blind when he assisted
at the inquiry, and thus made what Mr. Perceval,
the Prime Minister, declared " was the finest
speech that ever issued from the mouth of
man." Its great merit seemed to consist in
the analytical power of the speaker, and the
felicity of his argument.

After listening with the most profound attention to the evidence, he caused it to be read
over to him, and he then proceeded to demons-
trate that Mrs. Clarke had made twenty-eight
positive assertions, in some of which she con-
tradicted herself, and in almost all was contra-
dicted by unimpeachable witnesses. Out of
twenty who disproved her statements, thirteen
were persons of unexceptionable character.

Mr. Burton did not attempt to defend the
immoral connection of the Duke of York with
the woman who became the most prominent
witness against him, but he was desirous that
His Royal Highness should have fair play in
the investigation originated by Colonel Wardle,

and that he should not be convicted of con-
nivance at an illegal traffic upon such testimony
as his accuser was able to adduce.

The oratorical power and singular penetration
of Mr. Burton offered one more proof of the
truth of the frequently repeated remark that
Nature, in her compensatory arrangements,
often invests individuals who have been deprived of one faculty with an enlarged capability
in respect to the other senses. In the case
of Mr. Burton, the ear had received into the
mind all the facts which had been presented
to other hearers, while the eyes were denied
the advantage of physiognomical deduction;
but the mind had not been diverted from a
close and careful consideration of the serious
subjects it received by the contemplation of
external objects, and he was thus enabled to
arrive at just conclusions, which probably
escaped the ken of those judges of the Duke
whose attention had been distracted by a
multitude of other considerations.

CHAPTER VI.

—

RESIGNATION OF THE DUKE OF YORK—STATE OF THE ARMY
UNDER HIS ROYAL HIGHNESS—GENERAL SIR DAVID DUNDAS
—NEW SYSTEM OF MANŒUVRES—THE REGENCY—THE DUKE
OF YORK—SIR HENRY TORRENS—TRIAL OF GENERAL WHITE-
LOCKE—GENERAL SIR HARRY CALVERT.

CHAPTER VI.

THE resignation of the command by the Duke of York was a source of poignant regret to the whole Army. His Royal Highness had done so much good and acquired so perfect a hold upon the affections of officers and men, that his departure from the Horse-Guards was regarded as a great calamity.

General Fitzpatrick, being asked what state the Army was in when the Duke of York took the command, said, "He was persuaded that there was no officer of long standing in the Service who recollected the state of the Army previous to the Duke's assumption of the command, who would not readily testify to the very great improvement which the

Army had derived, in every respect, from His
Royal Highness's management of it."

The Secretary at War, General Grosvenor,
and General the Hon. Chappel Norton, all
spoke to the same effect. Sir A. Wellesley,
who on his retirement from India, had been
employed by the Duke in England, and on
the expedition to Copenhagen, likewise spoke
very warmly as to the effective condition of
the Army, and pamphlets were recalled to mind
in which strong testimony was borne to the
paternal interest invariably manifested by the
Duke in all that concerned the Service.

In Hood's "Treatise on Military Finance,"
which contains evidence of the Duke's intense
application and consummate knowledge of military
tactics, we find the following pages referring
to a General Order and regulation of a highly
beneficial tendency:—

"In this the soldier will find himself protected from every species of imposition, and
encouraged by every merited reward that can
stimulate a well-disciplined army to loyalty
and an intrepid discharge of their duty: on

the other hand, it will be observed, His Royal
Highness has taken effective means to guard
the public purse against the inroads of agents,
paymasters, clothiers, and military contractors
of every denomination, and that, too, with
such legal precision, that his rules and orders,
resemble equally the correct composition of an
able lawyer and the production of a skilful
general."

Upon the resignation of the Duke of York,
the King nominated General Sir David Dundas
to the Command-in-chief. Sir David was an
officer who had seen service, and had, moreover, distinguished himself as a theoretical tac-
tician.

A thorough conviction of the want and
the necessity of a permanent and general
system of discipline in the British Army
induced Sir David, in 1795, to prepare and
publish a volume embracing the Principles of
Military Movements, chiefly applied to Infantry,
illustrated by the manœuvres of the Prussian
troops, and by the British campaigns in the
war of 1757.

Then, as one hundred and fifteen years later, the Prussians were the great models for the English Army; but the wars of the French Revolution demonstrated that a more rapid system of movement, adapted to the formations of an enemy who knew the advantage of velocity of attack and the prompt acquisition of good position, was preferable to the Prussian method.

Sir John Moore, one of the best officers in the British Army, entirely disapproved of "Dundas's manœuvres," and applied to them an opprobrious epithet sufficiently condemnatory of their character.

The Army did not deteriorate under the management of Sir David Dundas. His manner was more formal than that of the Duke of York, and his discipline not less strict; but he qualified his personal demeanour and the rigidity of his rule with undeviating politeness, not unmixed with kindness.

His duties were heavy and anxious, for during the two years of his command Lord Wellington was fighting the battles of the Peninsula, and

required continual reinforcements of good troops
and the assistance of able Generals. On Sir
David Dundas rested the responsibility of supplying the former and selecting the latter, ex-
cepting when the Secretary of State grasped the
patronage in favour of his party.

The illness of the King necessitated the appointment of a Regent in the person of the
Prince of Wales. One of the earliest acts of
His Royal Highness was to restore the Duke of
York to the command of the Army. An enforced
absence of two years had taught the Duke the
importance of a more strict supervision in the
disposal of appointments and commissions, and
the necessity for great activity in supplying the
requirements of Lord Wellington, who had yet
three years' work before him, in clearing Spain of
the presence of French armies.

On resuming the command of the Army, the
Duke of York appointed Sir Henry Torrens, his
Military Secretary. The career of Sir Henry
Torrens was remarkable. It was an almost un-
broken chain of success.

After being educated at the Dublin Military

Academy, where the hilarity of his temperament procured him the sobriquet of "Happy Harry," he entered the Army in 1793, in the 52nd Foot. He was not then much above fourteen years of age. He soon afterwards went to the West Indies, and found opportunities of distinction which attracted the attention of Sir Ralph Abercromby.

On his return to England, his regiment was ordered to Portugal, as part of the small force under General Cuyler. He had not been long there, when the regiment was ordered to Holland, to share in the contest with the French Republicans.

During one of those unfortunate campaigns, in which the British reaped nothing but honour, Sir Harry was wounded.

In 1801 we find him in Egypt, in command of a regiment,—he being then but twenty-three years of age. From Egypt the corps went to Bombay, but the climate of India did not suit the constitution of Sir Harry, and he returned to England in ill-health.

In 1806 he was at Buenos Ayres, as Military

Secretary to the unfortunate General Whitelocke.
On the trial of that officer, Sir H. Torrens behaved with great delicacy. He could not defend
the absurd conduct of his chief, but he carefully
abstained from saying more than was absolutely
extracted from him by the members of the
Court.

The reputation he had made for himself led
Sir Arthur Wellesley (afterwards Duke of Wellington) to offer him the post of Military Secretary, on the occasion of Sir Arthur's proceeding
with a division to drive the French out of Lisbon.
That was in 1808.

On the supersession of Sir Arthur by Sir
Harry Burrard, and Sir Hew Dalrymple, the
hero of Roleia and Vimieiro, and the unwilling
associate of those officers in the Convention of
Cintra, resigned his command, and proceeded to
England, Torrens accompanying him.

Here the path of good fortune was widened
for Sir Henry. His Royal Highness the Duke of
York offered him the appointment of Military
Secretary at the Horse-Guards, on the retirement
of Colonel J. W. Gordon. He could not refuse

so honourable a position, and it was fortunate
for the Duke that on his resumption of the command he had so able a coadjutor in his bureau.

Sir Henry was indefatigable. Rising at 5 A.M,
he applied himself diligently to the performance
of his duties, which at that time were particularly onerous. The war with Napoleon taxed all
the efforts of the Horse-Guards to keep up the
supply of troops, and upon their return home it
was no light work to arrange the reductions of
the Army, and to place on the best possible footing the force which remained.

In 1819 Sir Henry Torrens, the better to carry
out his ideas of military reform, accepted the
appointment of Adjutant-General at the Horse
Guards, and in that capacity revised the old
Field Regulations, which had survived their
author, Sir D. Dundas, and were in force beyond
the period of their utility.

His Royal Highness the Duke of York generally showed great judgment in the selection of
officers to fill the higher Staff appointments. In
1799 he gave the office of Adjutant-General to
Colonel Harry Calvert.

Perhaps the connection which Calvert had
established with Mr. Greenwood, the Army
Agent, whose niece (Miss Hammersley) the
Colonel married, may have had something to do
with the appointment, for the Duke had, it is
believed, placed himself under pecuniary obligations to Mr. Greenwood. Be that as it may,
the selection of the Colonel was exceedingly
judicious.

The Adjutant-General, who afterwards became
General Sir Harry Calvert, had served in
America, and in Holland in the brigade of
General (Lord) Lake—the only two fields in
which officers at that time could reap distinction,
—and on the latter field he was one of the Duke
of York's Aides-de-Camp.

A biographer says of him that in the "important and arduous duties connected with his
Military station, and in those of domestic and
social life, his conduct was distinguished by
unaffected humility, unremitting diligence, disinterested integrity, and self-denying benevolence."

He died, September 4, 1826, and in a

funeral sermon preached by the Rev. H. Blunt,
the Vicar of Clare, it was said of him,—

" He was a man of the most perfect integrity
and the most inflexible uprightness and conscien-
tiousness,—in all the duties between man and
man blameless ; he ministered largely to the
wants of others, and sympathised most deeply
and most feelingly with them in their distress."

It must ever be a subject of pride to all the
British Army that so many of its superior
officers have borne high characters, not only as
soldiers, but as Christian gentlemen. Posthu-
mous honours may always be accepted as just
tributes to the virtues of the man the perpetua-
tion of whose memory is their object. Nothing
can be gained from him after his death. His
" dull cold ear " is deaf to fulsome praises, and
he has bequeathed no authority to his executors
to reward the authors of his epitaph in proportion to the exuberance of their eulogies.

The Duke of York was indefatigable in his
exertions to maintain the credit of the British
arms abroad, and ultimately had the satisfaction
to witness the favourable results of his conduct

in the destruction of Napoleon's second usurpation of the French throne. The triumph on the field of Waterloo would not have been so complete, had not the Duke sent forth the best troops then available for field service.

The war over, if he did not originate, the Duke cordially seconded all the measures that were passed for rewarding the efforts of the soldiers and their skilful and intrepid commanders.

CHAPTER VII.

GENERAL PEACE—ARMY AGENCIES—MR. COCHRANE JOHNSTONE
—SINECURES AND PENSIONS—DISINTERESTEDNESS OF THE
DUKE OF CAMBRIDGE—INTERFERENCE OF THE HOUSE OF
COMMONS—MILITARY COSTUME—CAVALRY CLOTHING BOARD—
THE POOR BLUES—JAPANNED HELMETS.

CHAPTER VII.

A ND now came a long period of tranquillity
in Europe. Bruised arms were hung
up for monuments, and stern alarms were
changed to merry meetings. But it is questionable if the Army looked upon the visage
of war as equally "grim" with the aspect of
peace. There was an end to promotion and
prize. Reduction came with his shears, and
the half-pay list assumed larger proportions
than consorted with the ambition of many
of the younger men who had entered the
service just previous to the war with Napoleon.

Though the Duke of York had escaped to

a certain extent the penalty of his connection with Mrs. Clarke, the notoriety which
his pecuniary difficulties, arising from an unfortunate passion for the gaming-table, had
obtained, left him open to imputations of
favouritism in financial questions.

In the absence of any positive proof of a
tendency on his part to make a market of
the Horse-Guards, attempts were made to
get at the supposed facts by a side-wind.
Mr. Cochrane Johnstone, for example, brought
forward (July, 1812) the subject of Army
Agencies, contending that the country was exposed to great risk of loss in case any one of
them should fail.

By 'way of illustrating the danger, he
mentioned that whereas the house of Greenwood (now Cox and Co.) had the agency of
only twenty-three regiments when the Duke
of York was appointed Commander-in-Chief,
they had *now become* agents for one hundred
and seventy-six battalions out of two hun-
drey and eighty-four, besides fifteen regiments
of Militia and the different branches under

the Board of Ordnance. He showed that Mr. Greenwood received £80,000 a year from the Government for his trouble, and enjoyed other collateral advantages.

It happened, however, unluckily for Mr. Cochrane Johnstone's case, that according to the Hon. Charles Long, one of the Joint Paymasters-General, large balances were at that moment due to Mr. Greenwood, owing to the arrears of accounts and audit. This did not substantially affect Mr. Johnstone's argument, that great advantage accrued to Mr. Greenwood from the Duke of York's patronage, and there is no doubt that the facts disclosed operated prejudicially to the Duke.

At the period of which we are treating, the Government was unpopular. Even the great successes of the British arms in the Peninsula did not reconcile the people to the vast increase of taxation resulting from the prosecution of the war; and a knot of politicians, who made up by their absence of great senatorial ability by their

clamour, insisted on a reform in the State
expenditure.

Sinecures were closely scrutinised and pensions denounced. Particularly great was the
outcry against a pension that had been
granted to Colonel McMahon, a personal friend
of the Prince Regent. Wise men took time
by the forelock, and resigned their sinecures
before the shears were remorselessly applied
to them.

Among those dependents on the favour of
the Crown was the Duke of Cambridge. He
held the command of the Home District, which
yielded him £4,200 per annum and forage
for twenty horses. His appointment might have
been justified by the possible necessity for the
employment of the troops in England, but
His Royal Highness felt that it had dwindled
to a sinecure, and that it did not sort with
his dignity, nor was justified by his necessities
that he should continue to hold it, and he
therefore placed his resignation of the command in the hands of his brother, the Duke
of York.

The disinterestedness of the Duke of Cambridge was universally applauded, and Lord Cochrane, then a member of the House of Commons, moved for a copy of the letter of resignation, that the House might have an opportunity of recording its sense of the "truly noble" conduct of the Duke. Lord Palmerston, however, did not see that any special expression of the admiration of the House was called for, and the matter dropped.

There was a good deal of bit-by-bit legislation during the Peninsular War, and the Army came in for its share of the delicate attentions of the Senate. Notwithstanding the position and influence of the Duke of York, the House of Commons could not resist the temptation to assert its dominion over military affairs.

Not content with disputing the value of victories, criticizing sieges and other operations, the "Magnificoes" descended to the discussion of items of costume, and made annual introduction of the Army Estimates

the peg for their strictures. For instance, in
1813, when Lord Palmerston was Secretary
at War, a Mr. Bennet hauled the Board of
General Officers over the coals. He wished
to know who were the Military *arbitri ele-
gantiarum?*

"Who," he asked, "were the persons who
devoted their time and talents to the mode of
sticking ostrich feathers into Generals' hats,
fastening tags (aiguilettes) on the shoulders,
and arranging the other articles of dress?
He should rejoice in an acquaintance with
those military milliners who had so trans-
formed the Life-Guards.

"He had seen the body-guards of various
potentates, but neither in splendour nor
manliness of appearance could they be compared with those of His Majesty before the
late alterations of their costume. He did not
know whether any gentleman present had
seen them in their new dress, but certainly
nothing more stupidly foolish, nothing betray-
ing a more ridiculous taste could possibly be
imagined.

" The unfortunate Horse-Guards (Blues) were ordered to be sent abroad. Did any gentleman see them before they went? Nothing could be more absurd than these military changes; they were worthy of Grimaldi and D'Egville;* adorned as they were with their pantomimic pomp and feathers, they looked the Rinaldos of an epic poem. It might be said that fine troops at home were destroyed, and bad troops sent abroad."

The time was quite a new era with the Army. There was a cavalry clothing board appointed, with the Duke of Cumberland at its head, whose resolves were memorialized against by General Officers as absurd, and one of whose regulations was called "inflicting a cap on the Cavalry."

One leading proposition was to deprive the Dragoon of his boots, but the Duke of York cancelled the order and dissolved the Board.

Then came another Board, under Lord

* Famous pantomimists of the time.

Harington, rather more meritorious. As the former one would take away the boots of the Dragoon, the latter would deprive him of his breeches! Laughable as this seemed, it was the fact; the heavy Dragoon was to have on home service *white* worsted pantaloons, and in the field blue worsted dittos.

Mr. Whitbread, who was one of the great guns of the Opposition, pathetically spoke of "the poor Blues," who were sent off with little cocked hats which could easily be knocked off, while the Life-Guards were furnished with brass helmets of such a weight that they were an infinitely greater evil than the one intended to be remedied. In addition to this weight, they were furnished with a rivet and a screw for the purpose of keeping fast some ornaments, and which were so placed on the inside that if a heavy blow of a sabre fell on the helmet it must fracture the skull of the wearer; and yet it was all done for the *convenience* of the soldiers! He had been told, however, that, by the present

ridiculous manner of equipping the Cavalry
the Colonels pocketed £700 a year, and yet
the helmets were not of that use their author
pretended.

Then the saddles : that which the Horse-
Guards had was anything but a saddle ; " two
sticks and a bit of leather composed its whole
construction."

But the changes thus censured were not
without their champions and defenders. Lord
Palmerston defended the saddle ; it was a
foreign idea, was in use on the Continent,
and did not subject the horses to sore backs
as did the English saddle. He certainly preferred the old, japanned cavalry helmet to
the modern brass one; but on consulting a
cavalry officer, he found that the former in
hot countries cracked, and consequently in the
event of rain it was immediately destroyed.

He defended the substitution of worsted for
leather in the nether integuments, — the leather when wet was difficult to clean, the
worsted soon dried; it had been tried with
success in the Artillery Train.

The idea of a "japanned helmet" in India is calculated to startle the mind, in an age when the tide of human sympathy has set in rather strongly towards the East, and originated the sensible felt caps; but the Dragoons at the battle of Assaye wore the helmet, and for thirty or forty years the head-gear of the Cavalry and Horse Artillery was exceedingly oppressive.

CHAPTER VIII.

———

VOTES OF THANKS TO THE DUKE OF YORK—AN ANXIOUS
CRISIS—REWARDS TO THE ARMY—CHANGES OF COSTUME—
EVILS TO BE COMBATED—AUGMENTATION OF THE ARMY—
ADOPTION OF NEW FIELD EXERCISES—MATERIAL POINT
OVERLOOKED—DEATH OF THE DUKE OF YORK—THE DUKE
OF YORK'S SCHOOL.

CHAPTER VIII.

IN the midst of the acknowledgments and
congratulations called forth by the successes of the troops during the Peninsular
campaign, which terminated with the battle of
Toulouse, and the later triumph at Waterloo,
it was not forgotten by Parliament and the
country that very much was due to the indefatigable efforts of the Duke of York. He
used every possible endeavour to keep the
regiments on the Home establishment well up
to the mark, so that if reinforcements should
be needed, there would be no lack of efficient
troops to enable the Duke of Wellington to
carry out his plans for driving the French
armies out of Spain.

In 1814 the Duke of York received the thanks of both Houses of Parliament for "the benefits he had bestowed on the nation as Commander-in-Chief in the wars then concluded." In 1815 thanks were again voted, and allusion was made to his "continued, effectual, and unremitting exertions in the discharge of the duties of his high station, during a period of upwards of twenty years."

The call made upon the Duke's efforts when Napoleon landed from Elba was of a nature which it was as impossible to resist as it was difficult to obey. A war had broken out with the United States of America. Scarcely had the troops completed the task imposed upon them in the Peninsula, when they were shipped off to Baltimore and Washington, to win fresh laurels on the fields of Bladensburg, Chrysler's Farm, and other localities. The Duke of York was therefore compelled to fall back upon the Militia to swell the British contingent which was to arrest the course of Napoleon.

It was an anxious crisis. The Duke of Wellington sighed for his old infantry in the impending struggle, none the less that he had little faith in his Belgian and Dutch allies, and small hope from the British levies drawn hastily from the plough and the workshop.

But the Militia regiments gallantly upheld the national character. There was no flinching among them before the attack of the French Cavalry and the incessant thunder of Napoleon's artillery. They stood as if they were riveted to the earth, and contributed to the Duke of Wellington's resolution to hold his ground, if possible, until " night or Blucher " should come.

The labours of the Duke of York were in no degree lessened by the cessation of war, but their character was changed. He had now to reorganise the forces, more or less demoralized by seven years of campaigning, and to see to the distribution of rewards and alterations in the costume.

The rewards were not cast in a very

generous mould. The Order of the Bath was extended, a medal was issued to all of the " Waterloo men," colour-sergeants were created, the year 1815 was allowed to count as two years in the computation of the time requisite to entitle a soldier to a pension; ensigns of the Foot Guards were granted the rank of lieutenant, and the First Foot Guards were called the Grenadiers, and that was the sum-total of the recompense.

But plenty of work was cut out for the Army tailor,—

"That great enchanter, at whose rod's command
    Beauty springs forth, and Nature's self turns paler,
Seeing how art can make her work more grand."

Breeches and long gaiters which took a world of time to button were now superseded by Wellington trousers and boots, and shakoes were substituted for felt caps. A new form was given to cocked hats, and the infantry swords took a more formidable shape.

Linked by fraternal ties in war, where all are exposed to a common danger, the *esprit de corps* among officers is apt to grow weak

when the vulgar pleasures of a garrison town
pall upon the taste, and drive men to moods
of discontent. In default of healthy professional and other profitable occupation, the
turf, the gaming-table, and the billiard-table
become habitual *délassemens*, and load too
frequently to disputes, loss of money, and loss
of character. An undue degree of familiarity
is established between commanding and subordinate officers, and the bonds of discipline
become relaxed.

Against these evils of a "calm world" the
Duke of York had to combat, and sooth to
say, he found abundance of occupation in
revising courts-martial and publishing remonstrances. There was a serious misunderstanding in the 10th Hussars, which obliged the
Duke to remove nearly all the officers to
other regiments :—the Marquis of Londonderry
fought a duel with an ensign who had been
a cornet in his own regiment; Lord Carhamp-
ton brought Lieutenant-Colonel French, of the
6th Dragoon Guards, to a court-martial; two
officers of the Artillery were dismissed from

the service for refusing to participate in a Roman Catholic service; Colonel Bradley, at a West India station, was removed from the *Army List* for appealing to the House of Commons against a decision of "the Horse-Guards" in respect to a claim he had set up in opposition to another officer,—and many smaller matters engaged the Duke's painful attention.

On the other hand, he found much occupation of a general nature in procuring a large augmentation to the Army in 1825, which gave promotion without purchase to a considerable number of officers, whose advancement had been retarded through the accidents of service and their own slender means.

He further established a system in the sale of commissions which he hoped would have prevented collusion between buyer and seller in the matter of over-regulation prices of commissions.

At the instance of Sir Henry Torrens, who succeeded Sir Harry Calvert as Adjutant-General, the Duke of York sanctioned the adoption of new field exercises and manœuvres, in supersession of the Dundas scheme, which had failed to work satisfactorily.

Much, however, as the Duke of York had done for the Army, there was one material point which His Royal Highness had strangely overlooked. It never seemed to have occurred to him or any of his Staff that the soldier was much overweighted.

Taking the French and Prussian armies as models in the matter of costume, the Duke condemned the Infantry to a shako constructed in defiance of all the principles of architecture, and opposed to the dictates of common-sense. The crown was infinitely broader than the base which encircled the head, and as if that were not enough to assist apoplexy by conducing to pressure, massive chains and plates and a large tuft or hackle plume decorated the cap.

Then the men wore broad buff cross-belts, with a great brass-plate in front, bearing the number of the regiment. The pouch was ponderous, and never without a box for the regulation sixty-four cartridges. Heavy boots, and a large knapsack, containing many dirty articles required to keep the soldier clean, *id est*, brick-dust, pipe-clay, blacking, and their attendant sticks and brushes, and the usual changes of linen, shoes, &c., the knapsack itself being ingeniously strapped across the chest to impede respiration, completed the attire and its appendages.

No soldier equipped for the field carried less, when on parade in marching order, than eighty pounds' weight, Brown Bess and the bayonet included. In garrison his burthen was not under sixty pounds.

Foreign service made no difference in the costume and equipment. A regiment going to India was as well looked after in the matter of warm clothing as if the Arctic regions were its destiny; the thick black leather stock was as rigidly insisted on with the thermometer at ninety degrees in the shade, as if diphtheria would inevitably have been the fate of any soldier who had ventured to appear without it.

In June, 1826, the Duke of York was seized
with an attack of dropsy. The ordinary remedies
were applied, but he lingered for several months
in much agony. Still he did not relinquish the
fulfilment of his official duties, and so late as
the month of December he dictated all the
arrangements requisite to enable a Brigade of
the Foot Guards to embark promptly for Portugal in aid of our own little ally. The brigade
was highly efficient, and it was with no small
degree of justifiable pride that the Duke wished
that the country could compare its condition with
that of the brigade which landed in Ostend
thirty-two years previously.

On the 7th of January, 1827, the Duke of
York breathed his last, to the great sorrow of
the nation and loss to the Army. From first to
last he had ardently and consistently fulfilled
his duties. Though his views in respect to
military amelioration were large and general,
he was very attentive to details, not even the
most minute escaping his attention. He was
very frequently at his bureau at the Horse-

Guards, showing every consideration for the hard-worked staff and clerks.

Irrespective of the good work he had accomplished at the Horse-Guards, there was much in the manner of the Duke of York calculated to attach him to the men and officers of the whole army. He was courteous and friendly to all who had access to his person. He invariably returned salutes and replied to letters. When engaged on public business at the Horse-Guards, he usually dined there, and invariably invited the officer of the guard to his table.

He had frequent levées, whereat the ever ready kind word cheered the old, who had shared with him the dangers of the field, and encouraged the young, who were entering upon a new and possibly a glorious career.

But the best act of his military life was the establishment of the School at Chelsea for the reception and education of the sons of soldiers. To that institution the country owes a debt of gratitude, for it has produced a large number of trustworthy soldiers, and to this hour is a subject of pride among those who can appreciate

the moral training of boys, and cherish hopes
of their future good.   No spectacle is viewed
with greater public interest than a parade of
" The Duke of York's School," headed by their
own well-taught band of Lilliputian per-
formers.

CHAPTER IX.

ROYAL AMBITION—SIR HERBERT TAYLOR'S COUNSEL TO THE
KING—APPOINTMENT OF THE DUKE OF WELLINGTON—
GENERAL ORDER—OFFICERS OF THE STAFF—APPLICATIONS
FOR APPOINTMENTS—SIR WALTER SCOTT—COLONELCY OF THE
FOURTH DRAGOONS—THE CLAIMS OF SERVICE—THE DUKE'S
DISLIKE TO SOLICITORS—PATRONAGE.

CHAPTER IX.

THE appointment of a successor to the Duke of York was a source of some embarrassment to the King, George IV. Two of the King's brothers had occasionally spoken to him on the subject, but he was reluctant to give the command to either, and had more than hinted to the Duke of Wellington that, on the occurrence of the anticipated vacancy, he should wish to confer the office upon His Grace.

When, however, the Duke of York was actually called away, the King evinced a strong desire to take the Army into his own hands, with Sir Herbert Taylor, who had been the Duke of York's military secretary and confidential friend, as Adjutant-General, to com-

ı

municate his orders. But Sir Herbert was too
experienced an officer and too disinterested a
gentleman to allow the King to commit so grave
a mistake. He pointed out to His Majesty that
the Secretary at War being the Constitutional
Minister for the transaction of Army business,
it would be advisable to confer the appointment
upon a military man, thereby attaining the
double object of keeping within the constitutional
boundary and enjoying the official aid of a
soldier.

The King, however, objected. Sir Herbert
Taylor then submitted that it would be better
to appoint a Chief of the Staff in the person
of General Sir George Murray, who had been
the Quartermaster-General in the Peninsula.
But to this arrangement the King likewise had
a repugnance. The truth was, that he very
much desired to be absolute at the Horse-
Guards, and finding this to be impossible, he
consented to appoint the Duke of Wellington
to the Command-in-Chief.

That it might not be supposed he sought the
supreme command of the Army, the Duke of Wel-

lington had absented himself from London soon
after the death of the Duke of York. In a letter
to Mr. (afterwards Sir Robert) Peel, he stated
that the King had told him in the autumn of
1826 he would wish that the Duke should
succeed His Royal Highness, but the Duke
treated the conversation, " like many others, as
so many empty and unmeaning words and
phrases."

Nearly three weeks had elapsed, during which
the King coquetted with Sir Herbert Taylor,
and the General Orders were issued by Lord
Palmerston as Secretary at War. At length
the announcement of the Duke of Wellington
was made in the following words :—

" GENERAL ORDER.—The King feels that under
the present afflicting circumstances [the death
of the Duke of the York], His Majesty cannot
more effectually supply the loss which the nation
and the Army have sustained than by appointing
to the Chief Command of His Majesty's Forces
Field-Marshal His Grace the Duke of Wellington,
the great and distinguished General who has so

often led the armies of the nation to victory and glory, and whose high military renown is blended in the history of Europe.

    " By His Majesty's command,

        " HENRY TORRENS, Adjutant-General.

" Horse-Guards, January 23, 1827."

On the following day the King conferred upon the Duke the Colonelcy of the Grenadier Guards. The Duke lost no time in kissing hands and taking post at the Horse-Guards.

Sir Henry Torrens, the Adjutant-General, immediately sent the Duke a draft of the kind of General Order he thought he should issue upon the assumption of the command. The draft was full of compliments to the memory of the Duke of York, adding that he (the Duke of Wellington) would emulate his predecessor, in order to secure permanently the great objects favoured by the Duke of York.

But as the King had said a great deal about his lamented brother in the General Order which concluded with the appointment of the Duke of Wellington, the latter thought it would not be respectful to " obtrude his sentiments upon the Army in relation to their loss and his own." He declined, therefore, the adoption of Sir Henry Torrens' draft, and issued the following curt and characteristic order :—

" G. O.—In obedience to H.M.'s most gracious command, Field-Marshal the Duke of Wellington assumes the command of the Army, and earnestly requests the assistance and support of the General and other officers of the Army to maintain its discipline, good order, and high character."

With great good taste the Duke of Wellington continued the whole of the officers of the General Staff at the Horse-Guards exactly as he found them. Dr. Guthrie, the distinguished Army Surgeon, wished for the appointment of Surgeon to the Commander-in-Chief, but the Duke returned a negative to Dr. Guthrie. He said that he certainly should not appoint anybody without making the first offer to Dr. Hume.

"The fact is," said the Commander-in-Chief, " I have considered it a duty and a proper mark

of respect from me to my illustrious and lamented
predecessor to take his whole personal staff. I
could not think of omitting his surgeon from
among the number, although not personally acquainted with him, not only on account of his
own respectability, but his services to His Royal
Highness, and the regard in which he was held
by the Duke."

The Duke of Wellington had scarcely assumed
charge of the duties of Commander-in-Chief,
when he was beset by applications from members
of the higher class for the vacant appointments
within his gift. To judge from the tone of some
of his replies, it may be inferred that he preferred his own spontaneous selections to the
choice of officers recommended to his attention.

To Lord Melville he wrote on the 18th of
January, 1827 :—

"I wish I could convince my friend ——— that
he ought to rely upon his services and character
for advancement, rather than upon the private
solicitations of any one. He is a candidate for
the command at Chatham. I will only repeat to
you that I have known ——— above thirty years,

in service with the Army in different situations.
I don't believe there exists an officer more zealous
and able and conciliatory than himself."

But His Grace did not add, "and therefore I
give him the appointment."

Among the solicitors for patronage was Sir
Walter Scott. Writing to the Duke on other
matters, he incidentally said :—

"I am going to mention a circumstance which
I do with great apprehension, lest I should be
thought to intrude on Your Grace's goodness.
It respects a youth, the son of one of my most
intimate friends, a gentleman of good family,
who is extremely desirous of being admitted a
cadet of Artillery. His father is the best
draughtsman in Scotland, and the lad himself
shows a great deal of talent both in science and
the ordinary branches of learning.

"I enclose a note of the youth's age, studies,
and progress, in case Your Grace might think it
possible to place on your list for the Engineer
service the name of a poor Scotch hidalgo. Your
Grace knows Scotland is a breeding, not a feeding
country, and we must send our sons abroad, as

we send our black cattle to England; and, as
old Lady Charlotte, of Ardkinglas, proposed to
dispose of her nine sons, we have a strong
tendency to put our young folks 'a' to the
sword.' "

It is not improbable that, grimly smiling at
the pleasantry of Sir Walter, the Duke at once
placed the youth on the List, and perhaps had
him gazetted very soon. It was one thing to
get on to the Horse-Guards' List, and quite
another to be speedily removed from it to the
Army List.

Not so fortunate in his application was the
King himself. His Majesty had expressed a wish
that Major-General Lord George Beresford should
be appointed to the Colonelcy of the 4th Dragoon
Guards upon the occurrence of a vacancy. The
Duke replied by expressing a preference for Sir
George Anson.

Lord George had never seen a shot fired,—
Sir George Anson commanded a brigade of
cavalry in the Peninsula. Lord George had uni-
formly supported the Government in Parliament,
—Sir George Anson had as steadily opposed it.

The Duke was glad of the chance of showing how superior he was to all considerations but those which rested on good service.

He wrote to the King :—

"Your Majesty for seventeen years, and my lamented predecessor for thirty-two years, established the principle that the pretensions of officers to Your Majesty's favour should be fairly considered, notwithstanding their conduct in Parliament."

His Grace added that he should not wish to be supposed by the public to have forgotten all the claims of service, the examples of the Duke of York and the King's approbation, and to have departed from the example solely for the purposes of party and political influence.

In a letter to Sir John Malcolm, in 1825, referring to an application by an officer of the Royal Artillery to be appointed to a Captaincy of Horse Artillery, the Duke says :—

"I entertain a very particular objection to those officers who *solicit* favours, or require others to *solicit* for them. . . . . I am not to be *solicited* out of doing justice to all parties."

The Duke emphasised the word "solicit," because it had been used by the applicant, who believed that appointments were to be obtained by "solicitation."

In 1823, he thus replied to Sir Robert Williams, who had asked a favour for another person :—

" My patronage is supposed to carry something with it. If it does not, it is useless, and to grant it would be ridiculous. If it does, I ought, and must, take care not to grant it lightly. I ought to be well acquainted with the person to whom I grant it, and ought to be certain that he is equal to his competitors in his line, if not the best."

At a later period he answered Sir Herbert Taylor :—

" I cannot recommend Major B. for brevet promotion, without at the same time recommending a great many others, even if I thought the service rendered by Major B. was of a nature to merit such a mark of distinction. But I beg leave to add that I never recommended any officer to be promoted to brevet who had not distinguished himself in the field before the enemy *generally more than once,* and if only once, it must have been in a very extraordinary and conspicuous manner."

CHAPTER X.

THE DUKE OF YORK'S DEBTS—THE DUKE OF WELLINGTON'S
MEMORANDUM ON A PROPOSED SUBSCRIPTION FOR THEIR
PAYMENT—THE CANNING ADMINISTRATION—RESIGNATION
OF THE DUKE—ADMINISTRATION OF THE ARMY—SIR
HERBERT TAYLOR.

CHAPTER X.

VERY soon after the Duke's accession to
the Command-in-Chief, the Marquis of
Londonderry proposed a subscription for the
payment of the Duke of York's debts. On
this proposal the Duke drew up the following memorandum, dated the 2nd January :—

"The Duke of York is supposed to have
owed £200,000 at the period of his death,
for the payment of which no provision is
made. The honour of the family may be
considered as involved in the payment of those
debts. That point, however, must bo left
out of the consideration of this question.
The officers of the Army cannot be con-

sidered as the persons who ought to be
called upon to provide the funds for this
purpose.

"In respect to the lamented individual
himself, whatever may bo the degree of imputation resting upon him for incurring those
debts, without the means of discharging them,
it will still remain. What has passed is a
fact; and whether the debts are paid or
not, and by whomsoever paid, the fact will
continue to exist, and the imputation, whatever it may be, resulting from the fact.
The creditors, indeed, will be satisfied, and
their complaints will be silenced. So far
we shall hear no more of the fact of the
Duke of York having died leaving his debts
unpaid. But the fact will remain.

"Let us now see whether this subscription ought to be set on foot with a view
to satisfy and silence the creditors. Let us
only look at the situation of the General officers of the Army in general. There may bo
from a dozen to twenty of us capable of
subscribing a sum of money for any purpose.

But the great majority of the General officers have from £300 to £400 a year! How can it be supposed that men thus provided for can advance £300, or even £100, to pay the Duke of York's creditors?

" The distress of the creditors relieved (which by-the-by, it must be observed, has been occasioned by their own acts) would fall upon this meritorious body of men, who neither could nor would resist the call, if made upon them, whatever might be the distress it would occasion to them and their families. I am certain that if this question is fully considered, and the list of General officers is accurately examined by those who have moved in this question, they will find that I am right; and they will see that the distress of the creditors relieved by the subscription will be more than counterbalanced by the distress which the subscription will occasion.

"But this is not the only view of this subject. It is thought desirable that the officers of the army should manifest their attachment to the memory of their late deservedly lamented Commander-in-Chief. I quite

K

agree that the Army cannot manifest too
strongly its gratitude, its attachment to his
person and memory, and its respect for all
his measures and institutions. But in order
to attain this manifestation in reality, we
must take care not to propose to them measures which every man, or at all events the
great majority, will feel to be, and which
will be in fact, an exorbitant tax upon the
scanty means of subsistence which he pos-
sesses for himself and his family.

"It is true that this measure will be cried
up by that which we all despise, the venal
Press, as the finest trait in the character of
the Army, the most marked instance of its
attachment, &c. But what compensation will
those cries be for the individual distress which
such a measure will occasion? I earnestly
deprecate it, and I may do it with the more
freedom, as there are two persons now alive
who knew that I was willing to come forward, if others would, to arrange the Duke's
debts some years ago, if he would have
allowed of their being arranged."

The debts of the Duke of York became a subject of public inquiry and discussion some five years later, when it appeared that His Royal Highness believed, upon his death-bed, that he made ample provision for the payment of those debts, for in his will, dated in December, 1826, he desired that his executors, Sir Herbert Taylor and Colonel Stephenson, would sell all his property, and "after payment of his debts and funeral expenses" hand the residue to the Princess Sophia of Gloucester, His Royal Highness's sister.

It appeared that the Duke of York had lent money and entered into bonds for his brother George IV., to a considerable extent, and the King had promised the Duke in his later moments that he would see all the tradesmen paid. The King had abundance of private property. Besides certain possessions at Windsor Castle, Brighton, &c., he had accumulated £600,000. But he had now taken up with the "good old gentlemanly vice," and was reluctant to part with a single shilling.

The debts of the Duke were certainly enor-

mous. The sum paid into the banking house
of Coutts and Co. amounted to £45,000 annually, chiefly the interest on bonds given for
losses at play, on the turf, &c. Still the
King had the wherewithal to pay them, without taking into consideration the property left
by the Duke of York and the value of the
diamonds of the Duchess of York, which had
somehow mysteriously disappeared.

After the first rush of applications for appointments was over, the Duke of Wellington
proceeded very steadily with his duties at
the Horse-Guards—which indeed were, for the
most part, mere matters of routine—until the
month of April.

At the time of his assumption of the Command-in-Chief, the Duke was a member of
the Ministry over which the Earl of Liverpool
presided. Suddenly, the Earl was smitten with
paralysis, and the King in some perplexity
sent for Mr. Canning, and ultimately empowered
him to form an Administration. But the Duke
would not serve under Canning, though he
had for some time been one of his associates

in the Cabinet. He therefore withdrew from
the Ministry, and at the same time threw up
the command of the Army.

This last proceeding excited some surprise
in the country, for as the Command-in-Chief
was not a political office, there appeared no
incompatibility between the Duke's tenure of
that exalted appointment and his continuance
in the Cabinet. To this view, however, His
Grace did not subscribe.

In the explanation which he gave in the
House of Peers as his reasons for retiring from
the command, he stated that the Office would
have placed him any day in communication
with the Prime Minister, that he would have
had no control over the Army, inasmuch as
the chief control was in the hands of the
Premier, while the Minister could not move
troops, make up his budget, or introduce
reforms, without seeking the opinion of the
Commander-in-Chief. The truth was, the
Duke was much piqued that he should be
under the necessity of holding intercourse, as
a subordinate, with Mr. Canning, for whom,

on aristocratic as well as personal grounds, he had no great liking.

No successor to the Duke of Wellington was immediately appointed. The business at the Horse-Guards remained in the hands of the Staff, the Secretary at War issuing all the requisite orders.

In the meanwhile, the King returned to his old fancy for the supreme command, against which Sir Herbert Taylor and other loyal and friendly advisers continued to remonstrate. Mr. (afterwards Sir Robert) Peel was as much excited as his nature would allow him to be by the King's fancy for supreme and direct military authority.

"I fear," wrote the agitated Secretary to the Duke of Wellington, "indeed I *know* that the King is *talking* of an agreement which is almost incredible; that he, the King, should personally command the Army. I hope he is only *talking* of it, and that he will never seriously propose anything so fatal to the interests of the Army, so pregnant with unceasing embarrassment to his Government."

During the entire period between the Duke of Wellington's accession in April, 1827, until his resumption of the command in August of that year, the Army was without a Commander-in-Chief. The Secretary at War was the virtual head, and to keep matters as straight as they could be, Sir Herbert Taylor was appointed Deputy to the Secretary at War.

How the arrangement worked is best described in Sir Herbert Taylor's own words. In a private letter to the Duke, he says,

"We do want you here sadly; we want you, were it but to stem the torrent of military reductions with which we are threatened, and to place, or rather to maintain that question upon the proper footing."[*]

---

[*] On the accession of George IV. to the throne of England, the Duke made choice of Sir Herbert Taylor as his Military Secretary, in succession to Torrens. Sir Herbert Taylor had long been known to the Duke of York, and was in fact his Private Secretary from 1799, when he was the Duke's Aide-de-Camp in Holland, until the year 1805, when the blindness of George III. rendered it necessary that he should have a private secretary to read to and write for him.

Strongly recommended by the Duke of York for his fidelity,

intelligence, and high gentlemanly bearing, Sir Herbert Taylor was placed near the person of the King, and continued his Secretary until the insanity of the monarch caused the establishment of a Regency in the person of the Prince of Wales. The Queen was then appointed the special Guardian of the King. Her Majesty continued Sir Herbert Taylor as her own Private Secretary, but on the Queen's death, in 1818, he was thrown out of employment. It was, however, but for a very short period, for on the King's death, on the accession of George IV., he became, as has been said above, Military Secretary to the Duke of York.

On the withdrawal of the Duke of Wellington from the Horse-Guards, Sir Herbert Taylor intimated his intention of going abroad to reside; but he had so thoroughly acquired the confidence of the King and Royal Family, that George IV. appointed him "First and Principal Aide-de-Camp."

On the return of the Duke of Wellington to office, in the Autumn of 1827, he accepted the office of Surveyor-General of the Ordnance, and on the death of Sir Henry Torrens in 1828, he became Adjutant-General of the Army, retaining the appointment until 1830, when William IV. made him his Private Secretary.

On the death of the King, Sir Herbert Taylor retired into private life, and carried out his long desired purpose of living on the Continent. He died at Rome in 1839.

The qualities of Sir Herbert Taylor endeared him to his family, and in fact to all classes of society, from Royalty downwards. He was peculiarly amiable, and his manners very ingratiating.

CHAPTER XI.

———

CHAPTER XL

ON the 8th of August, 1827, Mr. Canning died, and Lord Goderich was called upon by the King to form a Ministry. The obstacle which the Duke had himself offered to his holding the Command-in-Chief now being removed, it was fully expected that he would resume the office.

His brother, Lord Maryborough, wrote to him on the 15th of August :—

" The general impression is that the command of the Army will be offered to you : the whole Army are in breathless expectation upon the subject. The language of the officers is that if you take the Command-in-Chief without any political situation, you will be the greatest man

in the world, and if you do not, there will be
nothing but despondency in the Service."

On the 17th of August, the King asked the
Duke of Wellington to take the command of the
Army again, and he did not refuse to do so.
The Army was for the moment proud that it
should be again under the Chief who had placed
it, by his achievements, "above all Greek, above
all Roman fame."

But old campaigners who were familiar with
the Duke's temperament and bearing towards
those who had followed him with zeal and confidence, did not feel perfectly at ease when the
appointment was announced. His temper was
irritable, his manner cold and reserved, his interest in the welfare of the officer and soldier
was supposed to have waned since he quitted the
Army of Occupation.

Court life and politics, it was said, absorbed
his attention between 1818 and 1827, and he
had come to be regarded by too many old soldiers
as a prominent figure in bygone military history,
whose bâton of Field-Marshal was shelved for
the term of his natural life. When, however,

it was announced that His Grace had, at the generous instance of Sir Herbert Taylor, selected Lord Fitzroy Somerset for his Military Secretary, the officers breathed more freely.

Lord Fitzroy Somerset had been the Duke's companion in arms since the first eventful expedition to Portugal in 1808, when "Sir Arthur Wellesley" superseded Sir John Craddock, and fought the battles of Roleia and Vimeiro. Lord Fitzroy was then the Assistant-Military Secretary and Aide-de-Camp of Sir Arthur. He subsequently succeeded Sir James (then Colonel) Bathurst as Military Secretary.

Lord Fitzroy came to England with Sir Arthur after the Convention of Cintra (which all England condemned, and Sir W. Napier defended in his *History of the Peninsular War*), but returned with him in 1809, when reinforcements were sent out after the retreat from Corunna. He was by the side of the Commander-in-Chief of the Allied Armies of England, Spain, and Portugal, in all the battles from 1809 until 1813—Busaco, Salamanca, Vittoria, &c.—and was wounded at Busaco.

In the battles and the subsequent sieges of
Ciudad Rodrigo, Badajoz, &c., Lord Fitzroy
Somerset exhibited the most brilliant qualities of
a soldier and the most perfect carriage of an
English gentleman.

After the war he returned home, and married
a daughter of Lord Mornington, the brother of
the Duke of Wellington, thus cementing his
close connection with his distinguished friend
and patron.

The return of Napoleon from Elba in 1815
again calling the Duke into the field, Lord
Fitzroy accompanied him, and at the decisive
battle of Waterloo lost his right arm. As long
as the Army of Occupation continued in France,
Lord Fitzroy remained as Secretary to the British
Embassy. On the evacuation of France, he was
made Secretary to the Master-General of the
Ordnance, and held that post until August,
1827.

No person of intelligence, writes one of the
numerous biographers of Lord Fitzroy Somerset,
could be habitually with so extraordinary and
eminently gifted a man as the Duke of Wellington,

and be admitted into his confidence, without benefiting by it, or without acquiring additional knowledge and experience in all public business, and especially in military affairs.

It was the possession of these advantages, added to the benevolence of his nature and his popular and accomplished manners, that obtained for Lord Fitzroy in official intercourse so high a character for the correct and quick despatch of business, and for softening, as far as possible, pangs of disappointment felt when the result was adverse to the claims submitted. His decisions and intentions were allowed to be considerate, just, humane, and clearly expressed, and were therefore unusually final.

Lord F. Somerset possessed a reputation for courtesy and high-breeding which were effectual guarantees that even the most unexpected refusals would be conveyed in the gentlest manner. No one would care to see the Duke who could obtain a decision from the Military Secretary, and the Duke himself was never very desirous of being troubled with cases and applications which his *alter ego* could settle in his name.

As Sir Herbert Taylor lost the appointment of Military Secretary, the Duke of Wellington made him his Adjutant-General, in succession to Sir Henry Torrens, who died on the 28th of August, 1827.

Sir Willoughby Gordon was appointed Quarter-master-General, and the Staff of the Horse-Guards was otherwise satisfactorily filled up by the appointment of Colonel Macdonald as Deputy-Adjutant-General, and Sir R. Downes Jackson and Lieutenant-Colonel Freeth as Deputy Quarter-masters-General.

The appointment of Sir Herbert Taylor to the office of Adjutant-General left vacant that of Secretary to the Board of Ordnance (Surveyor-General), and as the Duke was Master-General, many applications were made to him, on behalf of candidates for the vacancy.

H.R.H. the Duchess of Kent wished the Duke to appoint her friend and major-domo, Sir John Conroy. The Duke declined to gratify Her Royal Highness in delicate terms :—

"I would beg to submit to Your Royal Highness that although the salary of the office has been reduced, and is at present little higher than that now received by Sir John Conroy, the business of the office is immense, and would require such constant attendance and attention from the holder of it, that Sir John Conroy could not render that service to Your Royal Highness which is so necessary to your dignity and comfort, if he were appointed to fill it. Under these circumstances, I confess that I had not thought of Sir John Conroy as a candidate for the office of Surveyor-General of the Ordnance."

To a General Officer who sought the office the Duke was less courteous. After rather a brusque exordium, His Grace wrote:—

"It is perfectly well known that I am not forgetful of those who have rendered services to the public under my directions, but that I make no promises. I will likewise add that I cannot suffer myself to be dictated to or influenced by complaints of inattention to services rendered, to make any arrangement

L

to fill any public office in favour of which
all the considerations do not combine which
ought to induce me to prefer such arrangement to every other."

Until January, 1828, the Duke of Wellington
performed the functions of Commander-in-
Chief conjointly with those which fell to him
as a member of Lord Goderich's Cabinet.
Early in that month, however, Lord Goderich
resigned the seals of office, and the King sent
for the Duke to form a Ministry.

Accepting the Premiership, the Duke found
it would be impossible for him at the same
time to hold the Command-in-Chief. He therefore offered it to Lord Hill.

"There is no doubt," said he, "that your
appointment will be highly satisfactory to the
country as well as to the Army; but it has
occurred to some members of the Government
that considering the place in which you stand
on the List, it is better, in relation to the
senior officers of the Army, some of whom
have high pretentions, that you should be
senior General upon the Staff, performing the

duties of Commander-in-Chief, rather than Commander-in-Chief."*

Lord Hill accepted the trust, although he had a month previously refused the Master-Generalship of the Ordnance, on the plea that he was not used to office duty, and feared that a permanent residence in town would injure his health.

Lord Hill was decidedly the most distinguished of the Generals who had served under the Duke in the Peninsula. His services in Portugal and Spain had been beyond all price. Individually he was beloved by the Army. When the soldiery looked upon him in the Peninsula they thought of "home," for he was the type of a country gentleman; homely, kind, frank, and courageous.

A very few words suffice to describe the management of military affairs under that distinguished soldier. The kindness of manner

---

* This distinction without a difference has been observed to the present time. It is probably meant as a sort of compromise with the Royal prerogative. The Queen is absolutely Commander-in-Chief.

which had endeared him to the army in the
Peninsula, still marked his bearing in his intercourse with all who had business to transact at
the Horse-Guards. Inflexible in the maintenance
of discipline, he was nevertheless merciful and
considerate towards all whose errors were
more the result of haste, temper, or in-
advertence, than a departure from principles
of honour.

In times of peace and leisure, officers are
more disposed to a laxity in the fulfilment
of duty than when engaged in the bustle of
a camp, and commanding officers have a
tendency to descend to trifling exercises of
authority for the want of something to engage
their serious attention. Others are prone to
interest themselves in the details of political
life, and take an active part in public differences
which place them in an attitude of hostility to
the Throne.

Lord Hill was very impatient of military
disloyalty. He had serious occasion to rebuke
Colonel Thomas of the 20th Regiment, for
suffering speeches offensive to the Throne to

be made in his bearing and that of his officers, at a Conservative gathering at Ashton-under-Lyne. He brought Colonel Brereton, the inspecting Field Officer of the Nottingham district, to a court-martial, for failing to afford the civil authorities the requisite military aid in the suppression of a riot.

But if he sternly repressed indifference when loyalty and professional duty demanded activity, Lord Hill was prompt to recognise good service, and strengthen the hands of officers who had difficult tasks to perform. Riots and discontents in Canada, a negro mutiny in the West Indies, agitations in Ireland, disturbances in Birmingham were cases in point where the support and approbation of the Commander-in-Chief were essential.

CHAPTER XII.

SALE AND PURCHASE OF COMMISSIONS—OVER-REGULATION
PRICES—PATRONAGE OF THE ARMY—THE MARQUIS OF
LONDONDERRY—THE ROYAL HORSE-GUARDS, BLUE—MANAGE-
MENT OF THE ARMY—DEATH OF LORD HILL—CORPORAL
PUNISHMENT—REWARDS FOR GOOD CONDUCT.

CHAPTER XII.

THE abolition of the sale and purchase of military commissions which had frequently been mooted, even in the last century, was again brought forward after the Duke of Wellington had left the Horse-Guards in 1828. But he did not take the less interest in the subject in his retirement. On the contrary, we find him, in 1830, sending forth a very interesting and exhaustive minute or memorandum, in which the question is examined in all its bearings.

The following short passage sufficiently denoted the inclination of his opinion :—

"It is the promotion by purchase which brings into the Service men of fortune and

education,—men who have some connection
with the interests and fortunes of the country
besides the commissions which they hold from
His Majesty.   It is this circumstance which
exempts the British Army from the character
of being a 'mercenary army,' and has rendered
its employment for nearly a century and a
half not only not inconsistent with the constitutional privileges of the country, but safe and
beneficial.

"On the other hand, an examination of the
detailed operations of the system of promotion
by purchase, or the remuneration given by
the public to the officers of the Army for
their service, will show that those who purchase
their commissions, which are certainly three-
fourths of the whole number, receive but little
for their service besides the honour of serving
the King."

But the Duke was nevertheless much opposed
to the Over-regulation prices paid for Commissions.

In 1824, the Duke of York consulted him
as to the general question of the sale of

Commissions. Sir Herbert Taylor sent a series of interrogatories, and it was in this wise that the Duke of Wellington replied on the Over-regulation :—

" I would recommend to His Royal Highness to *declare* to the Army his determination to recommend to His Majesty to cancel any commission granted for which it shall appear that the officer appointed to it has paid more than the regulated price : and to dismiss from H.M's Service any Colonel or commanding officer of a regiment who may have forwarded or recommended such appointment, knowing that more than the regulated price has been, or was to be, paid for it."

The recommendation was not adopted because the Duke of York thought that nothing would be gained by the declaration, seeing the great difficulty of proving whether the injunction against over-payments had been obeyed. It was not very complimentary to the integrity of the Army to suppose that the truth would be withheld, but the Duke of York was tolerably correct in his conjecture. Declarations " on

honour," accepted *pro formâ*, generate a lax
morality, and in the Army these nominal
avowals had become so common, that officers
seemed to forget the meanness of the false-
hood they too frequently involved, in the
absence of any apparent peril to their pecuniary
interest. Probably the Duke of Wellington
became equally alive with the Duke of York
to the embarrassment attending the enforce-
ment of any regulation regarding extra-payments
for Commissions, for it does not appear that
during his long tenure of the command of
the Army he deemed it advisable to issue any
"declaration" of the nature he had suggested
to his predecessor.

Honoured with the confidence and approbation of the Queen and the countenance of
his old chief, Lord Hill's tenure of the command
of the Army was far from disagreeable to him.

The patronage of the Army in those days
was considerable. There was no troublesome
Staff College to levy contributions upon the
understandings of ambitious soldiers; no examinations for first commissions restricted the

choice of youth who aspired to the epaulette.
A Commander-in-Chief was not bound to give
away commissions according to the standing
of young men in the Horse-Guards' List. Conservative Members of Parliament, old friends,
the offspring of brother soldiers and unfortunate
widows, all found the way open to their solicitations. This made things pleasant, often at the
expense of justice.

Then the Colonelcy of the "Blues" was
given to Lord Hill, upon the resignation of that
appointment by the Duke of Cumberland upon
a point of etiquette,[*] and the sole command of
the entire Household Brigade was likewise
vested in the Commander-in-Chief.

The appointment of Lord Hill was a great dis-
appointment to the Marquis of Londonderry.
He had been feverishly anxious to obtain "The
Blues." Believing that the Duke of Wellington

---

[*] The Duke of Cumberland was "Gold Stick," and commanded
the Household Brigade, in virtue of that office. The severance
of the command from the official dignity was offensive to the
Duke's pride. It had "become a mere Court Office, which, as a
Prince of the Blood Royal, he could not hold."

would be glad of his political co-operation while
so much opposition was offered to the Duke's
Government, he fairly worried his friend the
Duke of Buckingham to intercede for him. He
pleaded his affection for the Iron Duke and
the Duke's supposed affection for himself. He
fidgetted about the claims of other officers.

"I think," he wrote to his friend, "the
Duke, even if Murray is to succeed Hill [in the
command of the Army], would hardly give the
latter a cavalry regiment, he having so recently
received from the Crown the best military
government going—Plymouth."

Some weeks elapse, and no one gazetted.
"What can the Duke mean?" asks the impatient
sabreur.

At length it is formerly announced that
"General Rowland Hill is appointed Colonel
of the Royal Horse-Guards, Blue." The Marquis
is frantic. He writes bitter letters. Pathetically
he exclaims,—

"Mortifications and disappointments are stub-
born things to swallow, after a long series of
devotions to one shrine."

The Duke of Wellington vouchsafes no explanation. He simply hints that there are things a Prime Minister dare not do, and perhaps he felt that so palpable an act of favour to a partisan would have aggravated the hostility of the Press, already sufficiently intolerant of Tory rule.

Many improvements as to the condition of soldiers and officers were inaugurated by Sir Henry Hardinge, the Secretary at War, while Lord Hill was at the Horse-Guards, and it was naturally a subject of gratification to the latter that he was enabled to second the efforts of an old companion in arms.

But Lord Hill did not altogether, and at all times, repose upon a bed of roses. The importunities of sundry old officers who coveted colonelcies, good-conduct pensions, and Colonial or India commands, were a continual source of trouble to one who always endeavoured to act justly, and it was no slight addition to his annoyances that a distinguished member of the House of Commons urged his removal from the command of the Army, on the ground that he was politically opposed to the Whigs.

Mr. Wynne, one of the Ministry, stoutly resisted the proposal (which emanated from Mr. Joseph Hume), because of its interference with the prerogative of the Crown.

" The House of Commons," said Mr. Wynne, " by dictating to the Crown whom it should or should not employ, would arrogate to itself the management of the Army, *than which nothing could be more dangerous to the Constitution.*"

If Mr. Wynne had lived to the year ·1871, he would have seen that the House of Commons asserted its power at all risks on a matter vitally concerning the well-being of the Army.

The death of Lord Hill in 1842 again threw the command of the Army into the hands of the Duke of Wellington.

One of the results of the interference of the House of Commons was the reduction of corporal punishment in the Army. During the tenure of the office of Adjutant-General by Sir Herbert Taylor (1830), an order was issued restricting the number of lashes which Courts-

martial could cause to be inflicted on offending
soldiers. The limitation was still far in excess
of the maximum subsequently decreed, in
deference to public opinion, but it proved
sufficient to *encourage the perpetration of
crime.*

No one acquainted with the goodness of
Lord Hill's heart could suppose him indifferent
to the suggestions of humanity, but his experience had satisfied him that for ignorant men
who are callous, and whose minds were not
alive to the influence of moral precept, an
appeal to brute force was all that was left
to a commander for the preservation of discipline.*

His conclusions were unhappily borne out by
results. In 1830 there had been 655 floggings
and 2684 courts-martial; but three years later
the courts-martial were 5,472 in number, where-

* At the period in question, just forty years ago, no system of
rewards or any other kind of encouragement was held out as the
prize of good conduct. Education had scarcely been introduced
into the Army. No fines were levied from the drunkard, and
recruiting was carried on amongst the worst classes of society.

as the floggings had been reduced to 376!
Thus the maximum of crime kept pace with
the minimum of punishment.

But those were evil days for the soldiery.
The pensions were reduced to sixpence per
diem, and to make that affluent consideration
the more difficult of attainment the period
of enlistment was prolonged.

Lord Hill was always opposed to the promotion of men from the ranks to commissioned
rank. He was desirous of rewarding good
soldiers, and thought that might be done without depriving the Army of the non-commissioned
officers, whom he justly regarded as its back-
bone.

Besides, he knew that no officer could possibly
live upon his pay, and to expect a person
promoted from the ranks to possess any
separate income that would compensate for
the deficiency of the *solde* awarded by the
country was absurd.

Nor did Lord Hill believe that the soldiery
were so ready to yield deference to one who
had sprung from their midst, as to a gentleman

by birth and education who had purchased his commission, however suited the elevated private or non-commissioned officer might be by his professional knowledge and general good character.

In this opinion Lord Hill had been borne out by a vast majority of the most experienced officers and the sentiments of all the men. In ten years, partly preceding and partly during Lord Hill's command, one hundred and fifty-eight non-commissioned officers had received commissions—about sixteen per annum—but it had been deemed advisable to appoint them Quarter-masters or Adjutants in regiments other than their own.

CHAPTER XIII.

———

SIR HENRY HARDINGE—MILITARY MEASURES—INCREASE OF THE
ARMY—MILITARY PATRONAGE—MILITARY EQUIPMENT—SIR
JOHN MACDONALD AND SIR GEORGE BROWN—STAFF APPOINT-
MENTS—MAINTENANCE OF DISCIPLINE—MILITARY TRIBUNALS
—DUELLING FORBIDDEN—CORPORAL PUNISHMENT—REWARDS
FOR GOOD CONDUCT.

CHAPTER XIII

IT was fortunate for Lord Hill, and tended
greatly to augment his popularity, that
during his tenancy of the Horse-Guards, the
office of Secretary at War was filled by a soldier
of cognate sentiments and large experience in
war. Sir Henry Hardinge was an excellent man
of business, and if a strict disciplinarian, was
keenly alive to the wants and claims of the
friendless rank and file of the Army.

It is difficult now to say how many of the
excellent military measures which received Parliamentary consent between 1828 and 1842 were
originated by Sir H. Hardinge, or were inaugurated by Lord Hill and his admirable staff. ·
Suffice it that by their conjoint action many

important reforms were effected, and sundry important steps taken to clear the way for the numerous candidates for military employment. Eight hundred and fifty-seven officers who were on half-pay commuted their stipends for the regulation price of their commissions.

Limited enlistment was discontinued, that discontented soldiers who resorted to self-mutilation as a means of escaping service might be compelled to remain with their regiments, and perform the duties of scavengers.

An increase of seven thousand men to the Army strength was obtained, to keep down the disturbances arising from the contest for Parliamentary reform and the commotions existing in Ireland.

Rewards for distinguished services in the Army to the extent of £18,000 a year were granted by the House of Commons; military officers were allowed to draw their half-pay while holding civil appointments; the fees payable on Military Commissions were abolished;

libraries were established in the different garrisons; religious instruction was disseminated and encouraged, and punishments in military prisons of a degrading character were abolished.

Immersed in politics, opposing the Reform Bill in 1832, and successively the administrations of Lord Grey and Lord Melbourne,—supporting Sir Robert Peel in power, and contributing largely to the passage of two or three measures of vital importance* which he had always previously resisted—the Duke of Wellington, during the fifteen years which had elapsed since Lord Hill became the " General Commanding-in-Chief," had learnt that military patronage was an important auxiliary to the promotion of great political ends.

Accordingly, we find that, on his again becoming Commander-in-Chief in 1842, he made the partial sacrifice of the claims of merit to those of political or party interest one of the cardinal rules of his official con-

* The emancipation of the Roman Catholics and the repeal of the Corn Laws.

duct, thereby ignoring all the old professions
of 1827.

The absorption of his mind in political strife
had further begotten an indifference to all
suggestions for improvements or changes in
the arms, equipment, and costume of the
soldiery. He yielded a little in respect to
certain items in military uniform, because it
was agreeable to his Sovereign or the Prince
Consort, and occasionally a Colonel of the
Horse or Life-Guards was permitted to indulge
in certain little eccentricities respecting the
head-dress of the Household Cavalry, shifting
that article from the helmet to the bear-
skin, and back again, and there all alteration
ceased.

The Duke had won battles with the old
smooth-bore Brown Bess, weighty accoutrements, most uncomfortable chokers, suffocating
stocks, and burthensome, ill-slung knapsacks,
and it was his unalterable maxim that what
had been accomplished before could be achieved
again with the same instruments. He took
no heed of the progressive advance of Conti-

nental nations in the science of war, and
looked upon artillery as an inferior weapon
to the musket. He sighed for his old Peninsular infantry on the field of Waterloo. In
Sir John Macdonald and Sir George Brown
he had Adjutants-General who fell readily
into his views, and one of them at least was
as remarkable for the churlish repulse of in-
ventors as the Military Secretary was courteous.

In the distribution of the higher class
of Staff appointments and Honorary Colonelcies, the Duke of Wellington favoured the
Tory aristocracy and his family connections. The Beauforts, Westmorelands, and
Pakenhams, and all political adherents,
divided the *loaves* and *fishes* amongst them to
a very large extent, while the officers who
were notorious for Liberal opinions were left
out in the cold. Sir De Lacy Evans was passed
over sixteen times when there was a Colonelcy
to give away.

To do him justice, however, the Duke did
not disregard the pretensions of old officers

who had distinguished themselves in the Peninsula as Brigadiers and Regimental Commanders,
viz., Barnes, Fane, Halkett, Frederic Adam,
Maitland, Combermere, Paget, Colville, Brad-
ford, Nightingall, Arbuthnot, Samford Whitting-
ham, and others, all came in for Colonial, India
or Irish commands. He either appointed them
himself when he came into office, or procured
the nomination when the Duke of York
consulted him on the occurrence of vacancies.

In the maintenance of a severe discipline the
Duke of Wellington preserved the traditions
of his Peninsular command. Recommendations
to mercy rarely served the offender who had
been brought to court-martial, unless some
weighty political or family influence was brought
to bear upon the Duke's clemency.

He usually left the proceedings of courts-
martial to the Judge Advocate and the Military Secretary, and only interposed when the
ultima ratio was pressed upon him by the
distressed *aristocratical* relatives of the dismissed
or cashiered offender.

So jealous, however, was the Duke of the dignity of a Military tribunal and of his own prerogative, that he evinced great reluctance to comply with the warmest entreaties of his personal friends if an officer had sought the advocacy and protection of a barrister, or any other outsider, in the conduct of his defence. He thought that soldiers should rely upon the integrity of the members of their own profession, and leave special pleadings and forensic eloquence to the "lazy sons of peace."

In the year 1843, the second from the date of the Duke of Wellington's return to the Horse-Guards, a duel was fought between two officers, which terminated fatally for one of them—Lieutenant Colonel Fawcett, of the 55th. This circumstance following upon another duel, in which the Earl of Cardigan wounded a Lieutenant of his own regiment, exercised the British public to so great a degree that the Duke of Wellington, in concurrence with the Secretary at War, obtained the introduction into the Mutiny Act and Articles of War of a clause prohibitory of the duello, "a prac-

tice which was a violation of Her Majesty's
Orders, and a flagrant breach of the law of
the land."

If nothing else had been done to distinguish the
Duke as Commander-in-Chief, this measure alone
would have handed him down to posterity as
a humane Christian and a sensible soldier.
But there was another step taken three years
later which advanced him to the foremost
rank as a military philanthropist. His Grace
assented to the limitation of corporal punishment in the Army to the infliction of fifty
lashes.

To these salutary measures are to be added
the introduction of extra pay for good conduct, distinguishing badges to mark the meritorious soldier, annuities to deserving non-
commissioned officers, either while serving
or in the receipt of a pension; military savings'
banks, and medals for war services at various
times and in various places, dating as far
back as the year 1806, when the battle of
Maida was won against a superior French
force.

Properly speaking, this last measure is not to be placed to the credit of the Duke of Wellington, although it was carried during his exercise of the supreme command. In truth, he had always opposed himself to what he considered an injudicious and indiscriminate distribution of honorary rewards, and it remained for Sir De Lacy Evans and the Duke of Richmond to obtain for the Army of the Peninsula what it had so long coveted.

CHAPTER XIV.

ENCOURAGEMENT OF RECRUITING—NORMAL ARMY SCHOOLS—
EDUCATION OF OFFICERS—THE HORSE-GUARDS' SYLLABUS—
AMUSING ANECDOTES—AN INGENIOUS CANDIDATE—THE
CHARTISTS AND THE CHARTER—MILITARY ARRANGEMENTS
OF THE DUKE—DISMAL FIASCO OF THE LAMBETH POLI-
TICIANS.

N

CHAPTER XIV.

IN 1847, another step was taken to encourage recruiting and give instruction to the soldier. The term of enlistment was restricted to ten years, with the option to the soldier of continuing to serve for a further term for the sake of the pension.

A school was established for the instruction of Normal Army Schoolmasters; remissions were made in the purchase-money of land at the Cape, in Canada, and other colonies, and the sale of spirituous liquors in the barrack canteens was prohibited.

Desirous as the Duke of Wellington had shown himself of giving every advantage to those officers who "lodged their money with the Agents"—for he abhorred the idea of democratising the Army or advancing men from the ranks—it was with no little surprise and alarm that the parents and guardians of candidates were suddenly informed, some time in 1849, that British officers were for the future to be "educated." Any ignoramus who could just sign his name and put two and two together was placed upon the "Horse-Guards' List," if he could pay £840 for a cornetcy or £450 for an ensigncy.

But some *exposés* of woeful ignorance came home so directly to the Duke's sense of what was due to the country and the Sovereign, that he directed Lord Fitzroy Somerset to prepare and issue a Memorandum informing all existing and future candidates for Commissions that they must be prepared to pass an examination before sundry of the Professors at Sandhurst in History and Geography, Algebra and Logarithms, Euclid, French, and Latin, Field Fortification, Orthography, and Caligraphy.

The appearance of this Memorandum created

the greatest consternation among the candidates, their parents and guardians. At least one-half of the youths had received no more education than would have sufficed to enable them to take their degrees at Dotheboys' Hall. Others were masters of Greek and Latin, but had learned little or nothing else. French was at a discount; of History and Geography some had a dim idea; Algebra was an awful puzzle; Euclid was bewildering; and Field Fortification was nowhere.

Old officers and noblemen hobbled to the Horse-Guards to implore, protest, and remonstrate. Knowledge in the Army! Such a thing was never expected of youth in their time. To be courageous and obedient, and able to pay the mess-bill had sufficed for all purposes of victory over Napoleon's Marshals and the Princes and Chieftains in the East—more could not be needed.

But Lord Fitzroy was inexorable. He smiled, and told the alarmed and angry patrons of continued ignorance that a very few weeks and the outlay of a very few pounds to a "crammer" would suffice to qualify any youth for the terrible ordeal.

Not a few of the candidates withdrew their names or had them withdrawn from the List, and turned their attention to the rough pursuits in life in which reading, writing, and arithmetic, upon a moderate scale, were all that could or would be needed. The rest, with a few exceptions, resorted to the "coaching" system, thus giving employment to many University graduates, retired officers, and schoolmasters.

Lightly as the understandings and attainments of the young candidates were drawn upon by the "Horse-Guards Syllabus," the tax was yet too heavy for a considerable number of them; many were rejected altogether, and many more obliged to undergo a second trial before they were considered qualified to enter the Service.

History and Geography were the great bugbears. Rendered unattractive, or carelessly introduced at the several schools, the aspirants found it a hard matter to go through a new course of study.

Many amusing anecdotes are extant of the

strange replies given to Dr. Chepmell, the Examiner in History, by some of the youths who had not studied with sufficient attention his brief extract of the events occurring between the Siege of Troy and the Accession of Queen Victoria.

Geography was a greater stumbling-block than even the facts and chronology of History. The son of a baronet came to town crestfallen, and told his father, who anxiously awaited his return from Sandhurst on the steps of White's Club House, that he had been "plucked" because he did not know the locale of Fernando Po.

" Fernando Po!" exclaimed *pater familias,* " I don't believe there is such a place. But here comes G——," and as a Prince of the Blood Royal drove up in his cabriolet the Baronet called out,

" I say, G——, where is Fernando Po?"

" How the deuce should I know?" rejoined the Prince, driving off.

A familiarity with Field Fortification was tested by ground-plans and elevations of field works prepared at home—or said to have been prepared—by the adventurous youth. One ingenious candidate showed his tutor a section and elevation of a bastion, and the profile of a parapet which he proposed to take up as a proof of his skill in geometrical drawing.

" Oh ! those will never do," said the crammer, who was conscientiously anxious for the success of his pupils.

" I beg your pardon," replied the youth, " they have already been passed by a fellow who went up last month and is now gazetted !"

It was high time that the drawings were made in the actual presence of the examiner.

Imperfect as the ordeal confessedly was, and admitted to be so at the Horse-Guards, where it subsequently underwent serious modifications, it had effected great good in introducing the sound principle that military officers should be educated men. The thin edge of the wedge had been safely introduced, and time alone was needed, accompanied by a competitive system at the examinations, to ensure a supply of officers who would be as remarkable for their accomplishments as their predecessors had been for rough valour.

Courage is a noble and indispensable element in the composition of a soldier, but coupled with professional ignorance, it is as likely to peril the safety of armies as to promote their triumphs.

During the entire period of his command of the Army, only one occasion presented itself—and that neither a very remarkable nor a particularly trying occasion—for the exercise of the Duke's skill in placing troops in position under his immediate direction.

In the spring of 1848, some mad-brained politicians of the lower order conceived the idea of forcing a new Magna Charta upon the country. They caused a Petition descriptive of their purposes to be drawn up, procured the signatures of many thousands who could just write their names, and many more who, not being able to write, attached their "marks;" while other ingenious "Chartists" added hundreds of fictitious signatures, many of which were those of noblemen and statesmen avowedly hostile to the purpose of the petition.

This monstrous document was to be presented to the House of Commons by a half-cracked

Irish Member, supported by a mob of 20,000
ragamuffins, whose imposing presence it was
expected would strike awe into the hearts of
the Legislature, and force an acquiescence. It
was intended to assemble at Kennington Common, a large open space south of London, and
thence march in formidable procession to Westminster Hall.

Nothing but disturbance could possibly have
arisen from such a movement, and the Government were, therefore, determined to prevent at
least the march across Westminster Bridge.
With this view, the Police Force was largely
strengthened and judiciously distributed. To
add to the *posse comitatus*, many thousands of
householders and other respectable members of
society caused themselves to be enrolled as
special constables.

But it was upon the troops that the most
profound reliance was placed, and thus the
Horse-Guards became the centre of business,
and the Duke of Wellington the central figure
in the business. The troops immediately available were a detachment of Artillery, the House-

hold Cavalry, three battalions of the Foot Guards, the 17th and 62nd Foot, the 12th Lancers, and a body of Enrolled Pensioners.

Altogether 8,000 men were enrolled, and so placed by the Duke that scarcely a man was visible. Some were masked at Somerset House, the Houses of Parliament, the Bank, and the Custom House. Others were ambushed in houses on either side of the Thames contiguous to the bridges.

Had the Chartists carried out their purpose to the extent of entering London, "Up Guards and at them!" would have settled the whole affair in a few minutes. Happily the Chartists saw in time that "the better part of valour is discretion," and instead of marching from Kennington Common *en évidence*, they sent their delegate, Feargus O'Connor, to the House of Commons in a cab, with the monster petition which was civilly received and consigned to the ordinary limbo of such absurdities.

"In the name of the Prophet,—figs!" The grandiloquence of the Turkish pedlar's exordium and its insignificant sequence were not more

ridiculous than the pompous preparations of the
Lambeth politicians and their dismal fiasco.   But
for the Duke of Wellinton's strategy, however,
the affair might have had a more serious termination.   Europe was in a flame of revolution at
the time, and no one could foretell to what
extent the madness of discontent might have
carried agitators in England, had not the Government been forewarned.

CHAPTER XV.

—

CHAPTER XV.

TIME out of mind the Army has been the favourite object of the sartorial tastes of the heads of the establishment. A volume might be filled with an enumeration of the fluctuations in military costume from the time of John, Duke of Marlborough, to those of Arthur, Duke of Wellington.

The ultra-simplicity of the uniforms worn during the Peninsular War was exchanged for a gorgeous style of attire better suited to the lacqueys of a Court than for the veritable sons of Mars. The Staff, the Hussars, the Horse Artillery were covered with embroidery.

The cocked hats of Generals and their aides were as ponderous and as richly laced as

those wonderful affairs in which parish beadles
were wont to exercise their authority. Girdles,
sabrotaches, horse-cloths, sword-scabbards were
all clinquant with gold. Even the infantry
epaulettes exhibited a great affluence of bullion,
and their dress-coats had as much lace upon
them as would have swallowed up a quarter's
pay and allowances.

But the thing was too costly to last. First
the aiguillettes of the Generals and King's
aides-de-camp disappeared; then the rich undress
girdles went, and the terrible cocked hats
were shorn of their dimensions.

Not, however, until 1848 was any general
order published directing a considerable change
in the Infantry. In that year, the lace and
embroidery on infantry swallow-tails were
essentially diminished; blue frock-coats were
abolished, and a grey great-coat substituted.

The arrangement was not destined to last
very long. In a few years the red tunic displaced the coatee, the epaulettes were banished,
and the sash ceased to encircle the waist and

was transferred to the shoulder, when it passed gracefully across the chest, a leather waist-belt sustaining the sword. The chaco was reduced to a small mockery of a head-covering, and a short blue cloth mantle superseded the great-coat to be in itself eclipsed by a patrol jacket.

As years rolled on and the Duke of Wellington waxed feebler, he became less interested in the duties of Commander-in-Chief, and left nearly everything to the Military Secretary, Lord Fitzroy Somerset, and the Adjutant-General. Still he was constant in his attendance when a regiment, or a staff appointment of any value was to be given away, or his special sanction and sign-manual were required. [*]

* In his good working days he was unequalled for celerity. General Sebastiani, who was at one time the French Ambassador in London, told Mr. Raikes (author of a Diary, &c.), that he was enchanted with the Duke, whose frankness and activity in business were beyond all praise. His expression was—

"If I have anything to communicate to His Grace, I write to ask at what hour he will receive me. The hour is appointed. I find him punctual as the clock, and in half an hour he has heard

At 4 P.M. his horse was brought under the magnificent archway of the Horse-Guards by his old groom, and there were never wanting groups of the curious who loved to look upon the ancient "iron" warrior. To these he invariably addressed the caution :—

"My horse kicks."

That tendency to lash out the hind legs appeared to be peculiar to His Grace's chargers, and nearly cost him his own life on the evening of the battle of Waterloo. It is on record that as soon as he had dismounted, "Copenhagen," whom the Duke had bestridden the whole day, nearly dashed his master's brains out in an ecstasy of delight at being relieved of the burden he had borne for twelve mortal hours.

Incapable as he was every day becoming of performing the active duties of Commander-

my report, he has placed his finger on the point which has reference to himself, decided on the line which he feels authorised to take, and gives me an answer without any ambiguity. Thirty minutes with him suffice to transact what can never be accomplished in as many hours with our wavering Ministers of France."

in-Chief, the Duke was very reluctant to transfer the office to anyone else, and seemed a little uneasy as to his successor at the Horse-Guards, whoever he might be.

It was probably under the influence of some such feeling that His Grace was induced to suggest to the Queen that upon his (the Duke's) death, it might be advisable to place the command in the hands of the Prince Consort. A proposal had been submitted to Her Majesty, on the occasion of the death of Sir J. Macdonald, the Adjutant-General, perhaps by the Secretary at War, that a Chief of the Staff should be appointed, to combine the duties of Adjutant and Quartermaster-General.

The Duke was consulted, but though he decidedly objected to the combination of the offices under one head, he did not see that there would be any impropriety in the measure if Prince Albert, representing the Sovereign, would take the command on the occasion of the next vacancy. However, as the Prince Consort had the good sense to see

that his proper station should always be at
the side of the Queen, aiding her with his
counsel and influence, the proposal fell through,
and the future was left to take care of
itself.

In September, 1852, the Duke of Wellington
died at Walmer Castle, Deal, in the 84th year
of his age, full of honour. The nation decreed
him a magnificent funeral, and a tomb
in St. Paul's Cathedral, side by side with
England's greatest Admiral, "Nelson of the
Nile."

The selection of a suitable successor to the
Duke of Wellington was one of the most difficult tasks that has fallen to the Queen during
her eventful reign. Her Majesty could not
be said to suffer from *l'embarras de richesses*,
but "*le choix*" must have caused the Queen
considerable anxiety.

If the rank of the officers from whom the
selection had to be made were the sole consideration, there would have been little difficulty
in the matter. There were Generals whose
seniority gave them a title to profound con-

sideration, and others who had the plea of long
service and special fitness to urge.

Lord Combermere had been one of the Duke's
most favoured and efficient auxiliaries throughout the Peninsular War; Lord Fitzroy Somerset
had been the Duke's other self for many
years; Lord Gough and Lord Seaton [Colborne
of the 52nd, who turned the scale at Waterloo]
were soldiers who had seen much service in
many lands, and were held in honour by the
Army. And there was the Prince Consort,
whom the Duke had himself recommended as
his successor. But none of these officers ap-
proached the ideal Commander-in-Chief of the
British people or their Sovereign. The foremost
man in all the world had headed their Army
for a quarter of a century, besides leading
hosts into the field against the skilled Generals
of the most successful military power in Europe.
Were the soldiers he had bequeathed to his
countrymen to be thenceforth commanded by
an inferior General?

It had become—and continued—an axiom
that no training, no study, can form a great

commander. Genius and experience are the
true reservoirs of a General. He refers to them
for his resources and expedients. " The faculty
of commanding is more the effect of a happiness
than pains; a talent from nature, an emanation
of the mind, which like the poetical excur-
sions of the fancy, no art can supply, no
industry attain."*

In the midst of the Queen's perplexity, the
name of Lord Hardinge was suggested to her,
and it was at once decided by Her Majesty to
appoint him in defiance of the pretensions of
more seniority.

His career had been highly honourable and
successful. His genius, or quick perception,
had been invaluable at a critical moment at the
sanguinary battle of Albuera.† He had been

* " Rudiments of War," anno 1777.

† Nearly twenty years after the battle had been fought, a
controversy arose in a Military magazine as to the share which
Lord Hardinge had had in the battle. By some writers and
certain actors in the sanguinary strife the credit of the victory
was given to Sir Lowry Cole.

The true story, as related by Lord Hardinge himself, and
admitted to be true, was this:—

for years employed as Secretary at War. He
had thrown aside the paramount claims of
military seniority and official supremacy, when
Governor-General of India, to assist Lord

The 29th, 48th, and 57th Foot were, in a military sense, almost
exterminated by the fire of the French from their advantageous
position on the heights. The 57th had scarcely an officer left.
Hoghton's brigade was in such a crippled and exhausted state
that it could not be expected to hold the position it occupied much
longer. The Spanish troops could not be prevailed upon to move
up to the left of Hoghton's brigade. Starved and harrassed by
forced marches, no effort could be expected from them. Aber-
crombie's brigade was in support of Hoghton's left flank, and
thus the right flank was entirely exposed. . . .

In this desperate state of things, not admitting of delay, but
requiring instant remedy, Lord Hardinge, who was the Deputy
Quartermaster-General to the Portuguese Army under Sir Benjamin D'Urban, and only twenty-three years of age, rode up to
Sir Lowry Cole, and proposed to him to attack the enemy's
column with his division (the 4th), which he did, and thus gave
the victory to the English at a critical moment.

It should be added that Lord Beresford, who commanded the
force, and Sir B. D'Urban were both too far distant to allow of
their being consulted. It was "Hardinge's characteristic prompt-
ness and decision which saved the battle," said Sir B. D'Urban,
and it was Cole's movement "which converted a defensive battle
into an offensive one at an important moment, and obtained a
decisive success."

Gough with his counsel, and temper that gallant
soldier's dangerous impetuosity at the great
battles on the Sutlej. Further, Lord Hardinge
was known to have enjoyed the Duke of
Wellington's thorough confidence and respect.
No better man could be found. He was forthwith gazetted.

The task before Lord Hardinge was in one
sense difficult. His immense official experience
as Secretary at War for some years had made
him very familiar with the absolute condition
of the Forces, and he had seen enough of the
troops in India and since his return home to
be sensible of their requirements.

But he was sagacious enough to know that
every step he might take in a forward direction
would be severely criticised by his old com-
panions in arms, jealous of his elevation, and
too much wedded to old habits to be easily
reconciled to innovations.

Moreover, his Lordship felt that every departure from the Duke of Wellington's inert system
would be regarded as a reflection on that
war-tried and venerable chief, discreditable to

his heart, if not to his judgment. However, the interests of the nation were paramount in his mind to every other consideration; and after a few months of delay, devoted chiefly to inquiry and a general investigation of the business of the Horse-Guards, Lord Hardinge went to work with a will.

Lord Hardinge's personal Staff of course differed from that of his predecessor. The office of Master-General of the Ordnance was conferred on Lord Fitzroy Somerset, who about the same time accepted the Colonelcy of the Blues, vacant by the death of the Marquis of Anglesey. The appointment of Military Secretary was therefore, after the lapse of a few months, given to Major-General Sir Charles Yorke, an officer of experience, but of a different mould from Lord Fitzroy Somerset.

CHAPTER XVI.

MAJOR-GENERAL SIR GEORGE BROWN—GENERAL FREETH—
INQUIRY INTO THE STATE OF THE ARTILLERY—FORMATION
OF A CAMP OF INSTRUCTION AT CHOBHAM—FORCE AS-
SEMBLED—MANŒUVRES OF THE TROOPS—AGGRESSIVE MOVE-
MENTS OF RUSSIA—THE "SICK MAN"—ALLIANCE OF ENGLAND
AND FRANCE.

CHAPTER XVI.

THE general Staff remained the same. Major-General George Brown was the Adjutant-General, with Colonel W. F. Forster for his deputy. The "active and estimable" Major-General Freeth was the Quartermaster-General.

General Freeth was an officer of great experience in the department. He had gone through all the gradations of the office from that of Deputy-Assistant Quartermaster-General onwards, to the great satisfaction of each successive Commander-in-Chief, for nearly forty years, beginning in 1813, on his return from the Peninsula, and was, therefore, in every way

a most dependable officer.* He was a gentleman
in the highest sense of the word, rivalling
Lord Fitzroy Somerset in the courtesy of his
demeanour, and leaving nothing undone in his
official capacity.

The Adjutant-General was a man of a totally
different stamp. There is no sceptre less suited
to the government of the Army than a rod
of iron. Though camp life be rough, and
the trade of the soldier in relation to the
enemies of his country the reverse of gentle,
it has always been understood that courtesy
and chivalry are twin brothers.

This rule is particularly applicable to a state
of peace, and to the connection between the
officers of an army and their immediate official

* The heavy additional labour imposed on the Quartermaster-
General's Department by the Crimean War had its effect upon
the health and strength of Major-General Froeth. He felt obliged
to retire in 1855, carrying with him the respect and the regrets
of every gentleman and officer at the Horse-Guards who had
shared and assisted in his toil and could appreciate his worth.
His retirement was pronounced a "public loss." The Colonelcy
of the 64th Foot was conferred upon him in recognition of his
services.

superior. But General Brown did not under-
stand the importance of good-breeding. He
was not deficient in the better qualities of our
nature; he had a heart that could feel for
misfortune and poverty, but he did not
allow his sympathies to extend to his military
duties.

Brusque in his manner to applicants for small
favours, almost boorish in his rebukes, and
obstinately wedded to Regulation, however oppressive and in arrear of the age, he became
a terror to young officers, and the instrument
of pain and humiliation to the elders. "*Bewar
the bar*" might have proved as appropriate a
warning over the gates of the Horse-Guards in
his day as it was a suitable scroll on the shield
of Scott's Baron Bradwardine.

"Go back to your regiment, Sir!" in pe-
remptory tones, was the only reply often vouchsafed to applicants for an extension of leave.
"Don't bring that d——d nonsense here!"
was the only notice taken of any new inven-
tion in arms or modification of accoutrements.

The martinet derided the idea of improvement in the knapsack, and looked upon a proposal to abolish the suffocating black stock, which enveloped the soldier's throat, with as much horror as the courtier manifested when he saw the first germs of a political revolution in the substitution of shoe-strings for buckles at a levée or a drawing-room.

Useful as a Deputy Adjutant-General in adhering to routine, General Brown was quite beyond himself in a more responsible position. The atmosphere of the Horse-Guards was much clearer after the General had left to command a division of the Crimean Army.

Lord Hardinge had not been schooled in fields of battle without being sensible that a good park of artillery is indispensable to success in war. So far back as 1828 he had been called upon to afford a Committee of the House of Commons the value of his testimony as to the condition of the British Artillery, and the opinion he then expressed had undergone no change.

On assuming the command of the Army, his
earliest step was to look into the state of the
Artillery. He found that there were scarcely
fifty guns in the arsenals available for service,
a number far below the proportion which the
rules of war decree that the ordnance should
bear to the infantry.

Mr. Sidney (afterwards Lord) Herbert, who
had become the Secretary at War, addressed
himself to the repair of the deficiency, and
brought his own military studies to bear in
the cheerful support he gave to the Commander-
in-Chief.

The musketry of the Infantry equally claimed
attention with the Artillery. The wretched old
smooth-bores had been superseded by a rifle
carrying a bullet invented by Captain Minié,
of the French Army.

After a time, however, the Minié ball, or
at least the cup of the ball, was declared to
be useless. Lord Hardinge lost no time in
substituting for it a conical bullet, cast at the
Enfield factory. Its value was tested a few
years later in the field, and gave to the

P

British Infantry a decided advantage over the enemy.

With the exception of the ten or fifteen regiments which had been engaged in the campaigns in India, China, Affghanistan, and the Cape of Good Hope, the British Army had been comparatively inactive since the close of the war with Napoleon I. in 1815. Men and officers —the "cankers of a calm world and a long peace"—were equally ignorant of field movements on a large scale and all the requirements of camp life. It would have been hazardous to expose them suddenly to the exigencies of field-service in their then state of unpreparedness.

To remedy, as far as possible, this state of things, Lord Hardinge proposed that a Camp of Instruction should be formed in a convenient locality, and when the House of Commons had voted the Estimates, a sum of £12,000 to £16,000 was allotted to the formation of the camp and its attendant expenses.

Chobham, in Surrey, was selected as the

head-quarters of the encampment. There were some thousands of acres of heath and common in the vicinity, suited to every variety of manœuvre with the three arms of the Service, and there, accordingly, in the summer of 1853, the force assembled for training and exercise.

The summer of 1853 received so large an amount of attention from Jupiter Pluvius, that the manœuvres at Chobham were carried on under great difficulties. The tents were soaked, so were the clothes of the soldiers. The little fosses formed round the tents to carry off the rain were filled to overflowing.

But the troops persevered in the operations, and every advantage was taken of a gleam of fine weather to go through a field day on an extensive scale. The men showed considerable skill and alacrity in hutting themselves and raising camp kitchens, sentry-boxes, &c., out of the brushwood and earth available, and on the whole imparted a confidence to the country that they would not be found

P 2

wanting when their services might be needed
in the field.

Lord Hardinge had the satisfaction of seeing
that the steps he had taken to improve
the Artillery had already. proved of service.
A Military correspondent of the " *United
Service Magazine,*" writing from the camp,
said :—

" Chobham has already had great beneficial
results for the Artillery. We have observed
with much pleasure that the waggons do not
go scampering after the guns, that there
is far greater steadiness in the fire, and
that the Foot Artilleryman handling his
9-pounder gun begins to take an interest
in what he knows is his own peculiar
weapon.

"However, within the last twelvemonth a
very great amount of amelioration has taken
place in this branch of the Service, and in
noticing its present defects, we do so with
the full hope that they will not escape the
attention of those who have it in their power

to make the British Artillery as perfect as
the rest of the Army."

Lord Hardinge had not introduced his reforms or encouraged the Army in field exercises
one hour too soon.

In the summer of 1854 it had become necessary for England to coalesce with France in
presenting a check to the aggressive movements
of Russia upon Turkish territory. The Emperor Nicholas made no secret of his purposes.
He believed Turkey to be in a drooping condition, and therefore an easy conquest. He
described the Ottoman Empire as " a sick
man " past hope.

But a pretence for war was wanting, and
this he professed to find in the refusal of the
Sultan to make amends for declining to interfere on behalf of the Greek priests in their
quarrels with the Latins, regarding the disap-
pearance of a silver star from the roof of a
chapel at Bethlehem.

Nothing would have been more easy for
Russia than to have poured her armies into

European and Asiatic Turkey, and possess
herself of Constantinople, despatching her
ships-of-war to the ports on the southern
shore of the Black Sea and the coast of
Syria.

The accomplishment of this object, however,
would have been fatal to the commerce and
the political prestige of England and France
in the Mediterranean. Neither Power, single-
handed, could have coped with the Autocrat
of All the Russias. An alliance between the
two ancient foes, to which Turkey and Sar-
dinia were parties, consequently became necessary.

The selection of the quota of troops which
England was expected to furnish devolved on
Lord Hardinge. There was no time to lose.
Already had the Russian armies reached the
left bank of the Danube, and essayed to obtain
possession of the Turkish fortresses.

So far they had been checked by the courage
and resolution of the Turks, not unaided by
British officers who had volunteered their
scientific aid. But a prolonged resistance

was not to be expected from garrisons weak in number and ill-furnished with artillery. It was necessary to forward an expedition at once.

CHAPTER XVII.

CHAPTER XVII.

MUCH enthusiasm prevailed on the subject among the British troops. A desire to cross bayonets with a Russian army had long been popular. Not that any personal dislike to the nation existed, nor that a particular affection for the Turks had been cherished in the English bosom.

The feeling of hostility had arisen in India some sixteen years previously, when it was believed that the siege of Herat by the Persians was part of a Russian programme comprehending the invasion of the British possessions in Hindostan.

Russia was associated in the military mind with aggression which it became a duty to resist

and chastise. The troops, therefore, prepared
for the expected contest in Turkey with
alacrity.

Still, their numbers fell short of the amount
of force that would be requisite immediately, and
for the ultimate filling-up of the gaps that would
inevitably be caused by death and disease. The
Militia, which two years previously had been
augmented, was merely intended as a reserve or
nucleus of a defensive force. Men, however,
were now encouraged to transfer their services
to the Line in consideration of a liberal bounty,
and Ensigncies in the Line were given to any
three officers of the Militia who could bring two
hundred and twenty-five men from their several
corps.

In a few weeks between twenty thousand and
thirty thousand gallant soldiers were equipped
for the Anglo-French Expedition, and Lord
Raglan, formerly Lord Fitzroy Somerset, was
appointed to command the British force.

A separate body of foreign auxiliaries, composed of Italians, Swiss, Germans, and Turks,
was raised under the instructions of the War

Minister, and some cavalry was ordered up from India.[*]

But the force thus improvised, as it were, was altogether incommensurate with the demands upon it. The Ministry, it was said, with too much truth, had believed in peace until they drifted into war. They believed in a little war until they found it was a war of giants; they believed in a small expedition to the Hellespont, until they found a vast fleet in the Baltic and another in the Black Sea; and worse than all, the War Office believed in a small army until its head (Mr. Sidney Herbert) saw that army perish before Sebastopol from the incompetence of the military organisation, and had to replace that handful of heroes by a force twice as large and an expenditure of wondrous profusion.

It is not the purpose of this "Personal

[*] It was expected that as he had been the principal disciple and confidant of the Duke of Wellington, Lord Raglan would have carried with him into the new field for his talents some of the military attributes of his great chief. The expectation was in a measure disappointed,—" *Tel brille au second rang qui s'éclipse au premier.*"

History " to repeat a story with which every
English reader is more or less familiar. Let it
suffice that although the general objects of the
Allied Armies were attained, and the traditional
character of the British for valour and endurance was supported, some errors of judgment,
some shortcomings on the part of officers of
rank and position, disturbed the public mind,
and became subjects of official and Parliamentary
inquiry. To Lord Hardinge this was particularly mortifying. It was charged against him
that, in the distribution of his patronage, he
was more apt to be influenced by considerations of personal friendship and connections than
by a regard to the claims of service and
seniority.

It is certain that a sense of gratitude to the
East India Directors, for the manner in which
they had acknowledged his services in India,
induced him to yield much to applications from
that quarter for appointments in his gift; and
it was no less notorious that in the selection of
officers to fill the Staff appointments with the
force proceeding to Turkey, he paid consider-

able attention to the wishes of his friends. No fewer than sixteen appointments were distributed amongst two families distinguished in military circles.

No objections could have been taken to the fortunate recipients of the Commander-in-Chief's favour, if they had inherited the military talents as well as the names of their progenitors; but they were as yet untried men, and it was injudicious to ignore the pretensions of officers of some standing and experience in favour of protégés of no standing and no experience.

The miserable plight of the troops resulting from the terrible weather in the Crimea was of course ascribed to the incompetency of the Staff in failing to provide against contingencies it was impossible to contemplate, but it was not until the operations in the Crimea were at an end that public attention was directed to Lord Hardinge's choice of officers, and then the whole weight of Parliament's displeasure was invoked against two of the Staff, who on their return received distinguished appointments.

These were Sir Richard Airey and the Hon. Colonel Gordon.

Mr. Layard, then a Member of the House of Commons, was foremost in raising an outcry, and contended that the Horse-Guards had treated the House of Commons and the country with contempt in appointing Sir Richard Airey Quartermaster-General of the Army, while an inquiry was pending as to his conduct in the Crimea. He even voted against the paltry £100 good-service pension which had been assigned that officer.

Sir De Lacy Evans, who brought his own personal experience in the Crimea to the support of his complaints, was vehement in his censure of Colonel Gordon. Alluding to the general selections for the field staff, he said:—

"I have seen that when this country is involved in war the chief situations on the Staff, and in the most important departments of the Army, are forthwith filled from the desks of the Horse-Guards. The men who are to occupy almost every important executive office —at all events, the principal offices—on the

Staff are brought from their desks. I believe that some of the officers engaged in the present war in those departments had not been in the field for forty years, some of them had not seen service for a period of twenty years, and the greater part of them had never met an enemy."

The criticism of a captious civilian did not weigh in public estimation against the high character Sir R. Airey had established for himself among military men. They alone could estimate fairly the awful amount of labour and responsibility that had devolved upon him, and they were foremost to defend him from the attacks of Mr. Layard and a part of the Press.

His subsequent action, and the manner in which he acquitted himself as Governor of Gibraltar, overpowered the calumny of which he had temporarily been the object.*

* Another proof of the high estimation in which the military talents of Sir R. Airey were held is to be found in his appointment to the responsible post of Adjutant-General of the Army in 1871.

Q

The weight of public displeasure did not fall
exclusively on Sir R. Airey and Colonel Gordon.
The mistake which had been made in charging
the Russians at Balaklava with unsupported
light cavalry, causing the destruction of almost
the entire brigade, was vehemently denounced
by all classes.

Lords Lucan and Cardigan were men of unquestionable bravery, and were, therefore, only
charged with incompetency and error.   They
pleaded the instructions of Lord Raglan, about
which there had evidently been a misconcep-
tion.

Whether the misapprehension was justly as-
cribable to the two Military Peers could never
be satisfactorily determined, for the officer who
bore   the   mandate   of   the   Commander-in-
Chief (Captain Nolan) had been killed in the
charge.

The chief allegation laid at the door of the
Earl of Cardigan was, that though he was the
first "in" with the Russians, owing to his
position as leader of the brigade and to the
speed of his horse, he was the first "out,"

when he found that the enemy were too strong for his intrepid followers.

Some twenty years previously, Sir John Elley, one of the best cavalry soldiers the British Army ever possessed, remarked—

"Galloping up to an enemy, and coming quicker back again, is a Cossack mode of warfare I do not admire in regular cavalry."

And this view of the matter the military and other critics of the day joined in endorsing.

CHAPTER XVIII.

THE WAR DEPARTMENT—SIR WILLOUGHBY GORDON'S REPORT—
ROYAL COMMISSION—ADMINISTRATION OF MILITARY AFFAIRS
—CIRCUMLOCUTION AND RED TAPE—SECRETARY OF STATE
FOR WAR—PRACTICAL JOKING IN THE ARMY—THE ARTILLERY
—THE DUKE OF NEWCASTLE—LORD PANMURE—DEATH OF
LORDS HARDINGE AND RAGLAN—CURIOUS COINCIDENCE.

CHAPTER XVIII.

DOWN to the year 1854 the management of the War Department of the State had been on an unsettled and unsatisfactory footing. There were a Secretary *for* War and the Colonies, and a Secretary *at* War, who divided between them the political, financial, and administrative concerns of the country in reference to the Army and our hostile relations with other nations; a Commander-in-Chief, to whom was entrusted all the details of Army economy as regards the Cavalry and Infantry; a Board of Ordnance, who had separate control over the Artillery and Engineers; a Board of General Officers, who regulated the clothing; a Commissariat department, who took orders from

the Treasury according to circumstances; a
Medical department; a Clerical establishment; a
body of Pensioners, &c.

Nothing but confusion and delay could possibly come out of such a state of things. The
various departments were all independent of
each another, the Secretary of State (who had
the Colonies to look after) being paramount,
and it was only through his office that either
of the rest could obtain from the other what
they might reciprocally require for the despatch
of any great military measure.

So far back as 1810, Sir Willoughby Gordon
drew up a Report on the subject for the information of the Government, but no action
was taken, probably because a change while
a war was in progress was only calculated to
make confusion worse confounded. It might
be likened to the dangerous step of changing
front in the presence of an enemy.

Twenty years elapsed, and the same incon-
venience, arising from a divided responsibility,
still operating, a Royal Commission was appointed to inquire into the existing arrange-

ments. But before it could make its report the Ministry was dissolved.

The Commission, however, was subsequently reappointed, with Earl Grey, then Lord Howick, Secretary at War, as chairman, and it made a report in 1837.

But it really seemed as if the Government was afraid to touch the question. The requisite alterations were of too much magnitude, and perhaps would have raised up jealousies. Circumlocution and red-tape pursued in common a comfortable system of routine, and indulged in no particular expenditure of thought.

Besides, we were at peace with all the world, and the Duke of Wellington, who was potent at the time, was averse to change of any kind at the Horse-Guards. And so the management of military affairs continued without vigour or unity of purpose.

But in 1854 we had drifted into a war with Russia, and the muddle was becoming intolerable. Once more, therefore, Earl Grey ventilated the subject in the House of Lords.

He showed that it was impossible to separate

the Military from the Civil administration of the
Army, and although in theory the Commander-
in-Chief had the discipline in charge, it was
necessary for him to apply to the Secretary at
War for authority to prohibit men from wear-
ing their side-arms; also to reward by a
" good-conduct warrant" the meritorious soldier, as a means of diminishing corporal punishment.

The Duke of Newcastle, who held the office
of Secretary for War and the Colonies, justified,
in some measure, the then existing state of
things, and opposed the idea of a Military
Board, which Lord Grey had suggested.

Lord Hardinge was still more vehement in his
opposition to change. He stated "most confidently" that if the Legislature attempted to
limit too much the authority and power of the
Commander-in-Chief as regarded the management of the troops, they would " shake his
authority in such a manner as to produce
great difficulties in the event of our having to
carry on a war."

Lord Ellenborough saw the great necessity

for a simplication in the mode of administering
military affairs, but was adverse to all Boards,
citing his personal experience of the Admiralty
Board. "They appear to me," said his Lordship, "to be but an excuse for the want of
responsibility."

Lord Panmure urged the placing the whole
management of the Army in the hands of
a Secretary of State, without touching the
patronage of the Commander-in-Chief.

The result of the discussion was the separation
of the Colonial from the War Department, and
the appointment of a Secretary of State on the
principle referred to by Lord Panmure.

The Duke of Newcastle was the first
Secretary of State for War, and during his
tenure of the office and that of his immediate
successor, Lord Panmure himself (who had
formerly been in the Army), several important
military measures were carried into operation
by Lord Hardinge.

A Commission reported on the great question of Army Promotion, which resulted in
the abolition of general brevets and the intro-

duction of a system of selection for the highest
grades. It was decreed that no officer should
serve regimentally after he had passed his
sixtieth year.

A permanent camp of instruction was established at Aldershot, in Surrey, and the strength
of the regiments was augmented.

Whatever hopes the Duke of Wellington may
have entertained of raising the character of the
younger officers of the Army by the introduction
of a certain kind of education, he had not entirely
extinguished vulgarity and boorishness.

In 1854, Lord Hardinge had to take serious
notice of some coarse practical joking in the
46th Foot, which led to a court-martial on a
Lieutenant more sinned against than sinning,
and in the following year, notwithstanding the
grave remonstrances of the Commander-in-Chief,
similar conduct in the 30th Foot called for severe
reprehension.

These were among the *désagrémens* of official
life. On the other hand, Lord Hardinge had
the satisfaction of promoting to commissioned
rank for their services in the Crimea ten

cavalry and twenty infantry non-commissioned officers.

A very important step was taken by the Government in 1855, which placed the Artillery directly under the control of the Commander-in-Chief. The Board of Ordnance and the office of Master-General of the Ordnance were abolished.

Until then a sort of divided authority existed, which operated injuriously, in multiplying correspondence and references, and delaying business in great emergencies, and in giving the Artillery a secondary place in the esteem and consideration of the Commander-in-Chief. It was probably owing to this nominal separation of duties and interests, that officers of the Artillery and Engineers were rarely selected to command a force in which the different arms of the Service were associated.

It was never supposed that a Cavalry General could not command Infantry and Artillery, or an Infantry General set squadrons in the field; but the notion that an Artillerist could command an army of mixed forces was habitually derided until a Pollock marched into Affghanistan

and a Napier achieved signal successes in China,
India, and Abyssinia. That Napoleon was an
artillerist by education and early profession was
never considered a sufficient reason for believing
a scientific English officer capable of exercising
command on a grand scale.

The Duke of Newcastle, who, with the best
intentions and most indefatigable efforts, had
failed to satisfy the national expectation as
Secretary of State for War, resigned the appointment in 1855, and was succeeded by Lord
Panmure, who, as Captain Fox Maule, had, as
has been said above, at one time been in the Army.

The Duke of Newcastle, before the Secretaryship for War and the Colonies was merged in
the new office of Secretary of State for War,
had had the assistance of Mr. Sidney Herbert
as Secretary at War. That energetic Minister,
when disaster came, and our departmental
defects were forced upon the public notice, .
"stripped himself to the work of regeneration
with resolution and intelligence."

He remedied short-comings, took many wise
and good steps, and alleviated the sufferings of

the troops with large benevolence and kindly
feeling. But his services were temporarily
lost to the country on the creation of the
Secretaryship of State, for the separate office
of Secretary at War was then abolished.

The health of Lord Raglan had been so
seriously shattered by fatigue, exposure, and
anxiety during the siege of Sebastopol, that he
was obliged to relinquish the command of the
besieging Army before the object of the Allies
had been attained. He accordingly returned
home, but only to die.

Regretted Lord Raglan assuredly was, for
though he had disappointed the expectations
of the country as the head of the British portion
of the Expedition, his captivating manners and
integrity secured him a continuance of the regard
he had enjoyed from the hour when he was
attached to the person of the Duke of Wellington in the Peninsula.

Lord Hardinge did not survive Lord Raglan
for many months. Accelerated by the toil and
worry incidental to his official duties during
the whole of the Crimean War, his death took

place in the autumn of 1856. He had been an
indefatigable servant of the State, in a military
or political capacity, for over half a century,
and was followed to his tomb by the regrets
of many good soldiers.

It was rather a curious coincidence that the
two chief military offices in the State should
have been held, at one and the same time, by
noblemen who had been equally bereft of a limb
through the fortune of war. Lord Raglan and
Lord Hardinge had each lost an arm.

The apparent singularity of the circumstance
of their being at the head of the two chief arms
of the Service could scarcely fail of attracting
attention, and was even deemed worthy of a
small poetical tribute. Some one prevailed on
the editor of the *United Service Magazine* to
assign his largest type to the following *vers de
circonstance* :—

> " Of Briton's Force, one arm's conferred
> On Fitzroy Somerset ;
> Hardinge the other arm preferred,—
> Derby* his wishes met.

* Earl Derby was the Prime Minister—1852.

Such heroes 'twas but fair to shield
From loss sustained by shot:
In lieu of arms left on the field
Two other *Arms* they've got."

CHAPTER XIX.

—·—

THE DUKE OF CAMBRIDGE COMMANDER-IN-CHIEF—MILITARY
SERVICES—CONDUCT AT THE ALMA AND AT INKERMANN—
SIR HERBERT TAYLOR — SIR CHARLES YORKE — A LOOP-
HOLE FOR GOOD-NATURE—MAJOR-GENERAL WETHERALL—SIR
RICHARD AIREY.

CHAPTER XIX.

ACTING probably upon the advice of her most loyal counsellor, the Prince Consort, Her Majesty appointed His Royal Highness the Duke of Cambridge to command her armies immediately upon the demise of Lord Hardinge.

There were many circumstances in favour of the Duke of Cambridge.

He was the only son of a Prince who had attached the nation to himself by his excellent conduct through life. We have seen how disinterestedly he had behaved in 1812, in throwing up a command which had become a sinecure; but many years previously he had elicited expressions of

admiration from foreigners visiting at the Court
of George III.

"A propos des gens distingués," wrote
Madame de la Fitte to Miss Burney, "il faut
vous parler, ma chère Madame, de nos deux
jeunes Princes. Celui dont vous faites mention
[the Duke of Cambridge] est le plus joli, le plus
gai, le plus caressant de tous les héros de
dix-neuf ans. Comme une blessure* sied bien
à cet âge! Je l'ai vu souffrir des siennes, mais
il me semble qu'il en jouissait."

The Duke had been absent for many years
previous to the death of William IV. as Viceroy
of Hanover, but it was not forgotten that he
had always been a good soldier and attended to
the British Army.

In token of the prevalence of this sentiment,
an Asylum for Soldiers' Widows had been erected
by public subscription in Norbiton Park, the

* The Duke of Cambridge (Prince Adolphus) had entered the
Army as an ensign in his sixteenth year, and was engaged in the
first campaign in the Netherlands in 1793. He was wounded and
taken prisoner at Hondschoote. He was afterwards released and
sent home. In 1803 he went out to Hanover to direct the defence
of the Electorate.

Cambridge estate, in 1852, to commemorate his many good qualities. The Prince Consort laid the corner-stone, and the institution, which received the title of the "Royal Cambridge Asylum," has flourished as an abode for destitute old women whose husbands had served the State as soldiers.

The Duke of Cambridge *fils*, who now succeeded to the command of the Army, had received a thorough military education before he entered the Army. On completing his studies he was at first attached to a cavalry regiment; served in Ireland and at a station in the Mediterranean, and received his baptism of fire at Iukermann, behaving throughout that memorable day, and at the previous battle of Alma, with the hereditary courage of the Brunswick family.

If his nerves failed him for a moment in the heat of the severe contest at the head of his division, it was because he beheld some of his chosen friends and many of the men of the Coldstream, whom he well knew, falling around him, under the withering fire of the Russian infantry. The

heart must have been made of stone that could
have witnessed such a scene of slaughter and
desolation wholly unmoved. By common consent, however, the Duke's bearing before the
enemy did honour to his ancestry and his
own good feeling.

Upon his return to England he was appointed
Inspector-General of the Cavalry.

In selecting the Duke of Cambridge for the
responsible post of Commander-in-Chief, Her
Majesty exercised a commendable judgment.
There were, it is true, many General officers
who were the Duke's seniors, and had a world
of experience to their credit, of which His Royal
Highness could not boast.

On the other hand, he enjoyed the inestimable
advantage of being thoroughly independent of
all party and Parliamentary influence. His
position as a Prince of the Blood Royal
counterbalanced the objections to his junior
position on the Army List, and his personal
intimacy with the Sovereign offered a guarantee
that the political power of the Secretary of
State for the War Department would no

prevent the Queen from being placed in direct communication with her Army.

The Duke of Cambridge was exactly the man to realise the idea propounded by Sir Herbert Taylor in his evidence before a Committee of the House of Commons, more than a quarter of a century previously. Sir Herbert Taylor was always in favour of the existence of a Commander-in-Chief who had perfect access to the Crown. He said :—

" It would be extremely unsatisfactory to the Army if their business were thrown into what is called a Civil department; the Army would feel and consider that their claims were not put in the same light, and could not be so well understood by a mere civilian as by a military man. *The Army would always look forward to an officer high in rank and station as the individual standing between them and the Sovereign.*"

In the universal recognition of the propriety of Her Majesty's choice, the Duke of Cambridge felt that he might calculate on the advice and hearty co operation of all the General and

other officers whose experience was worth
consulting.

Sir Charles Yorke continued to hold the
post of Military Secretary, and was useful to
His Royal Highness in curbing the good-nature
which led the Prince sometimes to yield to
applications in opposition to rigid rules of
military government.

The *bonhommie* of the Duke, which, though of
a somewhat rougher cast, resembled the kindly
frankness of the Duke of York, was strongly
contrasted with the acidity of his Military
Secretary, who, when he was referred to, con-
trived very frequently to neutralise the action
of the young Commander-in-Chief by pointing
out the inconveniences, irregularities, danger,
&c., &c., of his Royal Highness's intentions.
And it was perhaps fortunate that the head of the
Staff had, in some things "a voice potential
double as the Duke's," for the *entourage* of
the latter was of a nature to lead him occasionally into scrapes.

Associated on familiar terms with many
young and not always discreet officers who

could not promptly realise the new position
which "P. G.," as they were wont to call him,
had acquired, the Duke was exposed to solicitations which it would have been imprudent to
grant, but which he had not always the moral
courage directly to refuse. " Go to Sir Charles
Yorke," was the loop-hole through which His
Royal Highness evaded the necessity for doing
what his judgment condemned and his good-nature
could scarcely resist. Exactly as Lord Fitzroy
Somerset softened the asperity of the Iron
Duke, Sir C. Yorke neutralized the exuberant
kindness of the Duke of Cambridge.

In the department of the Adjutant-General
the Duke had a representative and aid who
was an honour to the Service. Major-General
Wetherall was an officer of the Lord Hill type.
Well acquainted with his duties, which were
of course often of an onerous nature, he
knew how to temper the austerities of rebuke,
command, and resistance by the unostentatious
effusions of a good heart.

He had long lived in social intercourse
with a considerable proportion of the Army,

and as a regimental commanding officer had won
the affection of all his officers and men. If un-
wonted harshness was called for in the Adjutant-
General's Office, General (afterwards Sir George)
Wetherall had only to refer the subject to his
Deputy (Brown), who readily relieved him
of the irksomeness of reproaching error and
negativing application.

The Department of the Quartermaster-General
was presided over by Sir Richard Airey, of
whom respectful mention has already been
made.

The personal staff of the Duke consisted of
associates who were zealously devoted to his
person, and did him no discredit as officers
and gentlemen.

Thus sustained, everything promised well
for the rule of the Duke of Cambridge. He
had the regard and confidence of the Army,
and a strong *personnel* at the Horse-Guards
to carry out the details of his administration.

But his course was not destined to run any
smoother than that of the proverbial true love.

The now element which had been introduced into the Government of the Army turned out an unpleasant check-string.

Until the time of Lord Hardinge, and for two years later, the Secretary at War had been little else than the keeper of the public purse; but that officer had now expanded into a Secretary of State for the War Department, and assumed and exercised a power which essentially minimized that of the Commander-in-Chief.

With the Secretary apparently originated all the measures which were to render the force valuable to the country, while the duty of the Horse-Guards was limited to the regulation of promotions and of appointments of a secondary nature, and the establishment of a system of drill and discipline. Not a soldier could be moved, not an alteration effected, or a comfort administered which involved the expenditure of one shilling, unless it so pleased the Secretary of State. He was the prime originator, the Commander-in-Chief the instrument. The one pulled the strings, the other was the puppet who capered in obedience to their momentum. " Sir Abel Handy *invenit* — Bob Handy *fecit*."*

In one sense this arrangement was serviceable to the chief at the Horse-Guards; it relieved him of a weight of responsibility; in another, it was an offence to his pride and a derogation from his dignity.

The Duke chafed and champed the bit at first, for he naturally felt that something might be left to the discretion of the first officer in the Army—the Queen's confidential steward, her relative and delegate—but the Duke of Cambridge was too sagacious to place himself in opposition to a " constitutional " arrangement, and soon fell into the groove which had been cut out for him.

* See the Comedy of " Speed the Plough."

CHAPTER XX.

CHAPTER XX.

UNDER the dual system of military government it is extremely difficult for those
who are not behind the scenes to learn with
whom the authorship of the wholesome measures originates. Acting in concert, the several
authorities may fairly share the merit between
them, but it will sometimes happen that the
suggestions of the Commander-in-Chief are set
aside by the financier, while the devices of
the latter are sure to be carried out by the former,
willy-nilly. On some points, however, the influence of the Commander-in-Chief is obvious,
and of the credit which attaches to them no
one can deprive him.

Thus the Duke of Cambridge may fairly

s

claim that to him is owing the improved education of the officers and men; the formation
of the system of rifle instruction at Hythe,
the introduction of an excellent system of field
exercises and evolutions, a reduction in the
weight and number of the soldier's accoutrements, the substitution of a valise for the old
knapsack,* the encouragement of mark firing
and sword exercise, the practice of marching-
out, the examination of Captains and Lieutenants
preliminary to promotion; and if he did not
originate, he most warmly seconded and gave
substantial co-operation to the adoption of
gymnastics, the introduction of fines for
drunkenness, the construction of lodgings and
a hospital for the wives and children of the
soldiers at Aldershot, the establisment of soldiers'
gardens at Chatham, the instruction of soldiers
in trades, the opening of the School at Bath for
the daughters of officers, the formation of the

---

* When a new kind of knapsack—a great improvement upon
the one then in use—was proposed, some fifteen years ago, Sir
George Brown, the Adjutant General, pooh poohed it, remarking
that "the knapsack question was exhausted."

Coast Brigade of Artillery, the appointment of fixed Deputies Judge-Advocate, to facilitate the operation of military law, &c., &c.

The difficulties of the Duke of Cambridge's position have been in a great measure enhanced by the continual changes that have taken place in the War Office. However ready an officer Commanding-in-Chief may be to accommodate himself to a new system of military government in which he loses some of his individuality, his duties must be more or less onorous, according to the disposition of the Minister with whom for the time being he is expected to co-operate.

The Duke of Cambridge for the first two years of his command worked cordially with Lord Panmure. That nobleman going out of office with Lord Palmerston in 1858, General Jonathan Peel became Secretary at War, but before he had time to look about him Lord Palmerston returned to power in 1859, and appointed Mr. Sidney Herbert Secretary of State for War.

Here the Duke had a wonderfully active coadjutor. Mr. Sidney Herbert who had, though

s 2

a man of large fortune, made military affairs, and especially the condition of the soldier, his *métier*, so to speak, recast the entire system of Army enlistment; he greatly improved the sanitary condition of the troops at home and abroad, considering it "under the lights of science;" he advanced the education and well-being of the soldier, promoted, organised, and retrained the Volunteer force, reconstituted the Artillery on the principle of rifled ordnance, and reconstructed the fortifications on corresponding principles.

Unhappily his strength and health were not proportioned to his noble efforts and untiring good-will. He died in August, 1861. His memory is preserved in a "Herbert Testimonial," which took the direction of all others he would most have desired,—a convalescent hospital for soldiers, which bears his name; and in a statue of "Lord Herbert"—for he had attained the title—standing in front of the present War Office, the office he had dignified by his labours and accomplishments.

To Lord Herbert succeeded Sir George Cornewall Lewis, a man of great energy and a high sense of justice. In him the Duke of Cambridge found an earnest ally, who looked at military questions more from a statesman-like point of view than with an eye to details.

Like his distinguished predecessor, he held office for less than two years. Dying, his place was taken in 1863 by Lord de Grey and Ripon, who had acted under him in the War Department, and Lord de Grey and Ripon in 1866 gave way to the Marquis of Hartington.

That nobleman's tenure of office was singularly brief, for in a very few months a change of Ministry brought back General Peel.

To the General succeeded (1867) Sir John Pakington, who had held the office of Secretary at War in 1852. Sir John found matters in a very different condition from what they were in his noviciate, but with peculiar energy he addressed himself to them, and worked well with the Duke of Cambridge.

His Royal Highness had steered very clear of politics since his accession to the Command-in-Chief, but his sympathies were, wo believe, with the Conservatives. Peel and Pakington were, therefore, far from disagreeable co-operators.

However, another change of Ministry brought back the Whigs in 1868, and Mr. Cardwell became Secretary of State for War, which post he still holds. Under Mr. Cardwell strange organic changes have been wrought. The most important are now upon their trial.

Mr. Cardwell has had a most valuable guide in Sir Henry Storks, an officer of rare distinction and ability, who has filled many high offices with the greatest credit; and likewise in Sir Edward Lugard, with whose aid the affairs of the Army in Mr. Cardwell's hands have not wanted the elements of a military sympathy which has not always distinguished the school of politicians to which he belongs.

The establishment of the Staff College, as a further step in the very necessary education of the officers, was highly commendable, but its popularity has suffered by frequent departures from the implied conditions of an officer's success in the prosecution of his studies.

It was believed that the certificate of a *passed* student would have been not only a certain guarantee of his fitness for employment on the Staff, but the declaration of a positive title to the distinction, to the exclusion of all candidates who had not gone through the prescribed ordeal.

In too many instances, however, nepotism, Court and Ministerial favour, or personal predilections have overridden merit, and officers have gone to their graves without reaping a single advantage from the devotion of two years' time to the mastery of the higher duties of their profession. The promise kept to the ear has been broken to the hope.

And further, when an officer has been selected from the Staff on the strength of his certificates, his tenure of office has been limited to five years, at the expiration of which time he has been obliged to go back to his regi-

ment, to find himself among comparative stran-
gers.

It is certainly but fair that the chances of
professional advancement should be spread over
as large a surface as possible, in other words,
that all the officers in the Army who have
qualified themselves at the College, or otherwise earned a title to promotion, should have
an opportunity of getting on to the Staff,
but on the other hand, it is possibly dis-
advantageous to the public service to remove
an officer from an appointment in which he
has laboured to establish his usefulness, and
to consign him to a humdrum occupation in
which no scope is afforded for his ability. No
rule, perhaps, was ever more worthy of exception than that which limits an officer's tenure
of a Staff office to five years.

From the earliest hour of his assumption of
the command, the Duke of Cambridge manifested an anxiety to relieve himself of the
responsibility of selecting officers for the command of regiments and the performance of
higher duties. He endeavoured to place the

advancement of officers on such a footing as should give seniority a just proportion of advantages without interfering with the claims of merit, and in fact to diminish rather than extend his patronage. He was accessible to all classes of gentlemen, and had his ear ever open to fair representations of the wishes of his fellow-subjects.

Candidates for commissions who had had difficulties with the Examiners found him always disposed to an indulgent consideration of their respective cases, and he never made a special favour of giving the sons of men of respectable positions in life a chance of entering the Service. But this accessibility to applications opened the door to abuses.

CHAPTER XXI.

ARMY AGENTS—TRAFFIC IN COMMISSIONS—AN EXPOSÉ—THE
MURDER IN NORTHUMBERLAND STREET, STRAND—COURTS-
MARTIAL AND COURTS OF INQUIRY—THE CASE OF CAPTAIN
ROBERTSON—PUTTING THE SCREW ON—COLONEL CRAWLEY—
JUDICIOUS MEMORANDUM—LIEUTENANT-COLONEL DAWKINS.

CHAPTER XXI.

THE interference of Agents in the purchase and sale of military commissions has always been deprecated officially and connived at privately. It has been prohibited by Acts of Parliament, denounced in General Orders, and discountenanced in elaborate minutes and circular memoranda.

But Commanders-in-Chief and Secretaries at War have avoided taking public notice of this notorious misdemeanour on merely extra-judicial grounds; they have sheltered their collusion in the traffic under the plea of the absence of any direct information of its existence.

And this has not been forthcoming, because

the accessories before and after the fact have been mutually interested in the secrecy of the transaction. "A plague on't when thieves will not be true to each other!"

In 1859 an *exposé* took place, arising out of the failure of a body of commission-traffickers to make fair division of the spoil. It seems that an Army tailor heard that a gentleman wished to get a commission for his son, but did not know how to go about it. The tailor mentioned the circumstance to a firm of "Army" agents, who had not received the profitable and recognised dignity of "Regimental" agents.

These gentlemen agreed to procure the nomination of the candidate for the sum of £400, in addition to the £450 he was to pay for the infantry commission. They accordingly employed one of their coadjutors,—a gallant free-lance, who, on the faith of his services with half-a-dozen armies, had access to the Duke of Cambridge — to apply to have the youth's name placed on the Horse-Guards List.

There was no difficulty about the matter, for the Duke of Cambridge never hesitated to "book" any one for whose personal respectability a voucher was forthcoming : he would undergo the usual examination in his turn, and be gazetted on his passing. No influence could protect him from that ordeal.

In a short time the young gentleman's name appeared in the *Gazette*, and the joyful *pater familias* paid down the stipulated sum.

But now came the critical part of the business.

There were five brigands engaged in the transaction, and they disputed their several proportions of the plunder. One of them, who contended that he was entitled to the largest part of the spoil, was fobbed off with what betting men call a "pony," no more than twenty-five pounds.

Finding his remonstrance produced no more, he at once turned Queen's evidence, and apprised the Secretary of State for the War Department of the dreadful crime that had been committed. The Minister had no alternative but to prosecute all the parties, except the informer.

Mr. Edwin James, an advocate remarkable for his eloquence and his skill in convincing a jury, was retained for the prosecution in the Court of Queen's Bench. A conviction was easily obtained, and the culprits, a Jermyn Street tailor, and the two Army agents *participes criminis* in the negotiations, expiated their transgression in the Queen's Bench Prison, where they were detained for six months.

Their offence admitted of no palliation. It was no defence to say that others had perpetrated the same enormity time out of mind with impunity. They had been guilty of what the witty Frenchman considered worse than a crime. They had committed the terrible mistake of allowing themselves to be found out.

Another disquieting circumstance in connection with irregular influences at the Horse-Guards was the murder of a pseudo-Army agent and money-lender who had an office in Northumberland Street, in the Strand.

The agent had conceived an illicit passion for the wife of a cavalry officer who needed money or interest at the Horse-Guards. The officer's regiment was ordered to India. This was fatal to the hopes entertained by the agent of ultimately conquering the virtue of the officer's wife. He, therefore, asked an acquaintance to procure the Commander-in-Chief's permission for the exchange of the officer into a regiment on a home station. The acquaintance knew that the permission would not be granted. " Sail or sell " was the rule.

The agent then proposed to employ other means, and so far got the officer to believe in their possible efficacy as to lure him to Northumberland Street.

Getting behind him on the occasion of one of his visits, the agent, despairing of the attainment of his object in any other way, discharged a pistol at the neck of his visitor; but the ball missed the spinal cord, and the officer, alive to the attempt at murder, seized

T

a decanter and dashed out the brains of his
assailant.

The affair caused a good deal of discussion
at the time, and taken in connection with the
previous occurrence, had the effect of creating
in the Army a distrust of the irregular agencies.
It likewise augmented the wariness of the
Commandor-in-Chief.

Several embarrassing circumstances in connection with courts-martial and courts of inquiry
have tried the temper and tested the discretion
of the Duke of Cambridge during the last ten
years of his command.

In 1862, a Captain Robertson, of the 4th
Dragoon Guards, was tried by court-martial
and cashiered because he acted in conformity
with one clause of the Articles of War, and
violated the provisions of another. He refused
to fight a duel, and did not adopt the alternative dictated by Military Regulations. The
sentence was quashed at the instance of the
Judge Advocate-General.

It was evident, however, in the course of
the proceedings and the events preceding them,

that there was a strong disposition at the Horse-Guards to lean to commanding officers and to treat junior officers with asperity.

Before the trial, Captain Robertson was summoned to the Horse-Guards, and was told *at once* to decide between a court-martial or permission to retire from the Service. He was naturally alarmed at this *de haut en bas* procedure, and asked for twenty-four hours' time, to have an opportunity of consulting his friends. The reply was that the Horse-Guards would grant no delay. Captain Robertson was to decide *then and there.*

He then entreated to be granted an interview with Sir George Brown, who was commanding in Ireland, and the entreaty was peremptorily rejected.

" This," said a writer in the *United Service Magazine,* " might not have been intimidation, according to the literal acceptation of the term, but that it was putting the screw on and using pressure, no man in his senses could deny."

This was not the kind of action the Duke

of Cambridge should have permitted. It
furnished ground for the supposition that the
Staff of His Royal Highness could behave as
they pleased—an impression which later events
did not remove.

In striking contrast with the bearing of the
Horse-Guards in the Robertson affair, was the
conduct of the Duke of Cambridge in reference
to some unfortunate occurrence in the Innis-
killing Dragoons, then serving in India.

The regiment had somehow got thoroughly
demoralized. Courts-martial on non-comis-
sioned officers had been every-day affairs, and
the officers were not all on good terms with
each other.

It was in this state that Colonel Crawley, an
officer of high repute, found the regiment on
his assuming the command, and the restoration
of harmony and good order seemed quite beyond his power. He was not seconded in his
efforts as he should have been.

He caused the Paymaster of the regiment
to be tried by court-martial, and though the
issue of that event was fatal to the Paymaster,

the Duke of Cambridge saw reason to reprehend the Colonel and his Major.

A " Memorandum," ostensibly proceeding from the Duke, was issued. It was most honourable to the sound judgment, impartiality, and strict sense of justice of its author. No document ever proceeded from the Horse-Guards more calculated to promote discipline and restore good feeling. It was certainly conceived in a high tone of displeasure and embodied dignified rebuke, but took a hopeful view of the future of the erring officers.

Subsequent to the publication of this Memorandum, the Colonel of the Inniskillings was himself tried by court-martial and acquitted.

In his remarks on the court-martial — the proceedings on which, following military usage, were forwarded to England — the Duke of Cambridge maintained the same tone. Indignant at the conduct of the Major, the Adjutant and the Surgeon, he removed them all from the regiment, but he could not fail to perceive that there had been faults of command which it behoved him to notice.

"It is only," wrote His Royal Highness, " by a happy combination of temper, judgment, and discretion, united with firmness, that the command of a regiment can be properly conducted, and the more difficult the elements with which a commanding officer may have to deal, the more requisite is it for him to possess and exercise those qualifications of command."

All this indicated a praiseworthy disposition on the part of the Duke of Cambridge to uphold the dignity and interest of the Army, and serve the ends of justice.

Still the Duke of Cambridge could hardly shake off a liability to err from the gratification of certain personal partialities. As time and experience strengthened his position and consolidated his power, he seemed unconsciously to become somewhat more arbitrary in his decisions and less respective of public opinion.

Several cases might be cited in which His

Royal Highness's inclination to be just was counterbalanced by the fear of giving offence to old associates and friends.

The most striking was that of Lieutenant-Colonel Dawkins, of the Coldstream Guards, an officer of high honour and good service, and the son of an old soldier. It was charged against Lieutenant-Colonel Dawkins that he was infirm of temper, and the charge came from an officer who was by no means remarkable for the opposite virtue.

The Lieutenant-Colonel retorted with some statements reflecting on other officers of the Guards, which he was not entirely successful in establishing, and on this ground the affair was reported to the Duke of Cambridge by one of those mischievous institutions known as Courts of Inquiry—a species of Star Chamber, which the Duke of Wellington never would tolerate—that Lieutenant-Colonel Dawkins' continuance in the command of a battalion was not "beneficial" to the Service.

It now came to the Duke's turn to settle the question, and here he seems to have failed.

He admitted the high military deserts of
Lieutenant-Colonel Dawkins, who had served
meritoriously in the Crimea, said that nothing
he had done in the quarrel with Lords F.
Paulet and Rokeby (his senior officers) was
unworthy of a gentleman, and gave him the
option of retiring on half-pay or accepting a court-
martial! From this decree, as inconsistent as
it was severe, the Duke of Cambridge has un-
fortunately never swerved.

His Royal Highness was equally uncom-
promising in his bearing towards a Major Man-
sergh, who, after some years of suspension,
was restored to the Service by the fiat of Sir
George Cornewall Lewis.

CHAPTER XXII.

CHAPTER XXII.

TO the Duke of Cambridge is due the merit of abolishing in some measure the slow or ordinary pace in marching. It was a very popular kind of step in the days of the Duke of York, when the pompous movement of the Grenadiers of Frederic of Prussia was yet fresh in recollection, and it probably had its uses in accustoming infantry to the preservation of a careful alignment and a measured cadence.

It is an acknowledged principle in manœuvres that all the soldiers in a civilised army should keep to one uniform pace and time, so as to enable the commander of expeditions or defensive armaments to calculate the exact periods of the simultaneous arrival of troops at a given point, in view to the execution of a pre-concerted movement.

But there was no good reason for delaying to teach this important lesson through the medium of a quick step. It might have deprived the public of the edifying spectacle of Ensign and Lieutenant Broadlands, of the Grenadier Guards, who stood five feet nothing in his stockings and had £10,000 a year from his estate, making desperate efforts, at the risk of a rupture, to keep ahead of a company of stalwart rank and file; but beyond the luxury of the music of the "Duke of York's March," there was nothing worth preserving in the otherwise tedious "march-past." Continental troops—notably the Belgians, French and Germans—had taught us that the swinging trot is as efficacious for all purposes of war as the solemn tread regulated by the drummer's tap.

Although the correspondence of the Horse-Guards and the occasional levées and interviews vouchsafed to officers of all ranks engage a great deal of the attention of the

Commander-in-Chief, the Duke of Cambridge
makes a point of paying frequent visits to
Aldershot Camp, Woolwich, and the great garrisons of Chatham, Portsmouth, and Plymouth.

His Royal Highness's attention to details
is very remarkable. He has everything, down
to the most minute circumstances of a soldier's
life and condition, at his fingers' ends. And
more than this, he is a master of his business
in the field. No officer can handle troops
with more facility, no one is more quick, in
an impromptu sham encounter, in discover-
ing weak points and blunders.

This aptitude was particularly made manifest during the Autumn Manœuvres of 1871.
Many foreign officers were present, and each
unhesitatingly declared that the Duke of Cambridge thoroughly understood his business as
a General in the field.

In the transfer of the Government of India
from the hands of the East India Directors
to those of the British Ministry, an immense
addition of labour and responsibility devolved
on the Duke of Cambridge.

In the first place, he had to see to the equipment and despatch of a large body of European troops to India, to assist those on the spot in suppressing the Sepoy Mutiny. This alone involved a skill in organisation to which His Royal Highness had not been trained. But "worse remained behind."

The whole of the Indian Army was transferred to the Crown with the country, and although the internal management of the Empire and its military establishments was vested in the Secretary of State for India, the enormous increase of the permanent strength of the Royal Army cast upon the Horse-Guards a great augmentation of duty in the way of recruiting, correspondence with the India Office, selection of corps and staff officers of the higher grades, granting extensions of leave, and confirming promotions made by the Commander-in-Chief in India, to say nothing of revising the proceedings and rectifying, or otherwise, the sentences of general courts-martial. Nothing but unremitting care and attention on the part of the chief at tho Horse-Guards could prevent delay, confusion, and judicial errors.

No Commander-in-Chief in England had ever, perhaps, had so heavy an amount of business thrown upon his shoulders. And as if the addition in India of the quota of the augmented Royal Army (including several brigades of Artillery) were insufficient, a new element of anxiety was now introduced, not inseparably, but collaterally, into the functions of the Duke of Cambridge.

The Volunteer movement, originating in 1859, had rapidly assumed the proportions of a national institution, and as it was of questionable utility in its isolated and purely civic condition, it gradually fell under the notice of the Commander-in-Chief and formed on quiet field days an integer of a mixed force of many thousand men.

To deal with this new branch of the auxiliary force so as to promote its efficiency without exciting the jealousy of its chiefs, or trenching too much upon its notions of independence, was a troublesome task; but the

Duke of Cambridge managed to obtain its recognition of the authority of the Horse-Guards, and to secure its cordial acknowledgment of the interest he showed in its utility.

The Volunteers are now an admitted branch of the Army of Reserve, and there can be little doubt that if circumstances should at any time call that Army into the field, it will fulfil the expectations which have been raised as to its national utility.

No allusion has been made in the foregoing pages to the bearing of the Military authorities towards the public Press. The annoyances which the Duke of Wellington experienced during the Peninsular War, less from the criticisms of the journals than from the facilities they afforded the enemy for learning the dispositions and strength of his army, led to his remonstrating in his letters to the Secretary at War and Foreign Secretary, and to the disfavour with which he viewed the Press when he held office in England.

There are numerous evidences in his des-

patches and semi-private letters, however, that
he regarded the Press as the fair exponent
and organ of public opinion. We have shown
in a previous part of this Historical Sketch
that His Grace abstained from acts which he
otherwise might have perpetrated from an
apprehension that he would have excited the
surprise and displeasure of the country.

Lords Hill and Hardinge followed pretty
much in the wake of the Duke of Wellington.

The Duke of Cambridge has acted on altogether a different principle. Without courting
the support of the professional journals, he
accepted with good grace and practical acknowledgment the service which the *United Service
Gazette* was enabled to render him at the
commencement of his career at the Horse-
Guards, and he has ever since in his acts
and post-prandial public speeches acknowledged the value of well-conducted papers.

Lords Panmure and Herbert always admitted
the importance of a friendly alliance with the
military papers, and gave them all the advantage of early intelligence. We have before

U

us, at this moment, a letter from Lord Panmure of rather a striking character, elucidatory
of his appreciation of the good opinion of the
United Service Gazette.

One of his chief *employés* writes :—

(Private.)

"War Department, 12th January, 1856.

"Dear Sir,—Lord Panmure desires me to
say that he thinks it right to tell you, *before
it is publicly known*, that it is intended immediately to issue a Warrant, giving to the
Soldier the amount of Bounty which shall be
fixed *in money*, and providing him with a full
kit of necessaries at the public expense, instead
of, as at present, including the price of necessaries in the amount of Bounty authorized.
Thus the sum which will be advertised as
Bounty will be actually paid to the man.

"I am, Sir, yours truly,

"H. J. B. GASKOIN."

The measure originating with Lord Panmure
had a good effect on recruiting, but it afforded

more scope for dissipation, for the youngster joining could calculate exactly how much he had to spare for drink and other debauchery.

A better measure than this was the total abolition of the bounty, for which Mr. Cardwell and the Duke of Cambridge are to be credited. May they continue the good work it is in their power to perform, that in future editions of this PERSONAL HISTORY their names may stand out prominently among the best friends the Service ever possessed!

We commenced this Historical Sketch with a reference to the ugly old edifice in Whitehall called to this hour "The Horse-Guards." The career of its several occupants has been faithfully traced to the hour when the Military establishments, which had been separated for some years, were again brought together under one and the same roof in Pall Mall.

The leading idea in the transfer was the simplification of public business by bringing "the Duke" and the "Secretary" into closer communication. Seeing that the distance between the offices of the Commander-in-Chief and of the War Minister, when the former occupied Whitehall and the latter Pall Mall, was very slight, and communication by telegraph facile and frequent, it is not probable that much time and trouble has been saved by the process of removal.

Anyhow, little has been gained in respect to the architectural beauty of the bureaux. If old Buckingham House, where the duality now flourishes, is destined to become matter of history, the chronicler will find as little reason for praising the unadorned building in Pall Mall, as the most abject flatterer could ever have discovered in the "magnificent" Head-quarters of the Dukes of York and Wellington and their successors.

THE END.

824902

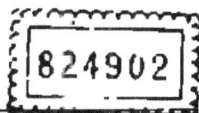

London · Printed by A. Schulze, 13, Poland Street.

MESSRS. HURST & BLACKETT'S
New Publications.

13, GREAT MARLBOROUGH STREET.

MESSRS. HURST AND BLACKETT'S
LIST OF NEW WORKS.

RECOLLECTIONS OF SOCIETY IN FRANCE
AND ENGLAND. By LADY CLEMENTINA DAVIES. *Second Edition.*
2 vols. 21s.

Among numerous other distinguished persons referred to in this work are :—Louis XVI, Marie Antoinette, Louis XVIII, the Duchesse D'Angoulême, Napoleon I, the Empress Josephine, Queen Hortense, Charles X, Louis Philippe, the Duke and Duchess de Berry, the Count de Chambord, the Emperor Alexander, King Frederic William, Prince Talleyrand, Prince Esterhazy, Blucher, Ney, Soult, Fouché, the Polignacs, Talma, Napoleon III, the Empress Eugenie, the Duc de Morny, Count d'Orsay, Victor Hugo, George IV, Queen Caroline, Prince Leopold, the Princess Charlotte, the Duke of York, the Duke of Wellington, Lord Byron, Sir Walter Scott, Sir H. Davy, Tom Moore, Mr. Barham, Mrs. Siddons, the Kembles, Mrs. Jordan, Miss Stephens, Mlle. Mars, Madame Catalani, Mlle. Rachel, the Countess Guiccioli, Lady Cork, Lady Blessington, &c.

"On proceeding to a conscientious examination of the contents, we found the familiar and commonplace matter lightened and relieved by many lively touches of description, many traits of character, many illustrative incidents, which may prove helps to history, and might have been irretrievably lost had they not been marked and recorded as they occurred. Lady Clementina Davies's opportunities were excellent, and the very traditions of her family are fraught with interest. Some of her local and personal impressions are as graphic and distinct as if they had been —so to speak—photographed on her memory."—*The Times.*

"The two entertaining and pleasantly-written volumes before us will interest and amuse many readers."—*Pall Mall Gazette.*

"Two charming volumes, full of the most interesting and entertaining matter, and written in plain, elegant English. Lady Clementina Davies has seen much, heard much, and remembered well. Her unique and brilliant recollections have the interest of a romance, wherein no character is fictitious, no incident untrue."—*Post.*

"A singularly interesting and amusing work, full of anecdote, gossip, and life. The entire record is full of entertainment."—*Sunday Times.*

"To every class of readers, Lady Clementina Davies's work will prove deeply interesting. As a book of anecdotes the volumes will be perused with avidity. Throughout the 'Recollections' we trace the hand of an artist, one whose power and talents are of the highest order, and who has the faculty of bringing before the reader the most striking incidents of the present century in France and England, thus combining the functions of the historian and the biographer with those of the delineator of life as it exists. The style throughout is terse and lively; it abounds with graphic descriptions, and there is an earnestness and a pathos when the authoress flies from gay to grave subjects that touches the heart. Witness the account of Josephine's sanctuary at Malmaison, and the dying hours of the ill-fated Duc de Berri. The lovers of history will be amply repaid by poring over the last days of Marie Antoinette at Versailles; the restoration of Louis XVIII to the throne of his ancestors; the escape of Napoleon from Elba; and the *Coup d'Etat.* The man about town will revel in those scenes in which Count D'Orsay, Byron, the poet Moore, Lord Petersham, and Sir Charles Wetherall took prominent parts. The patrons of the drama will have Catalani, Mrs. Jordan, John Kemble, the stately Siddons, Talma, Mdlle. Georges, Mdlle. Mars, Mdlle. Duchesnois, Miss Stephens, again brought upon the scene; the gossips will take in with avidity the small-talk of London society, the elopement at Paris; the eccentricities of Lady Cork; in addition to the above we have anecdotes of Walter Scott, Lord Fife, the Prince Regent, the Emperor of Russia, King of Prussia, Louis Philippe, Duchesse d'Orleans, the Esterhazys, Talleyrand, Napoleon I and III, Soult, Wellington, Esterhazy, and M. Thiers. No book of reminiscences has left upon us so pleasing an impression. It at once stamps Lady Clementina as a most agreeable and clever anthoress."—*Court Journal.*

1

MESSRS. HURST AND BLACKETT'S
NEW WORKS—*Continued*.

THE SWITZERS. By W. Hepworth Dixon.
Author of "New America," "Free Russia," "Her Majesty's
Tower," &c. *Third Edition.* 1 vol. demy 8vo. 15s.

Contents :—Mountain Men ; St. Gothard ; Peopling the Alps ; The Fight for Life ;
Rain and Rocks ; Teuton and Celt ; The Communes ; Communal Authorities ;
Communal Government ; Cantons and Half Cantons ; Cantonal Rule ; Canton
Zürich ; Pure Democracy ; A Revolution ; Popular Victories ; The League ;
The Federal Pact ; Jesuits ; Pilgrimage ; Convent and Canton ; St. Meinrad's
Cell ; Feast of the Rosary ; Last of the Benedictines ; Conflict of the Churches ;
School ; Democracy at School ; Geneva ; Schemes of Work ; Secondary Schools ;
School and Camp ; Defence ; The Public Force ; In the Field ; Out Again ; A
Crowning Service.

"Turn where we will there is the same impassioned eloquence, the same lavish
wealth of metaphor, the same vigour of declamation, the same general glow upon
the pages. Switzerland may be hackneyed as a country, yet there is freshness in
Mr. Dixon's subjects. Mr. Dixon throws a passing glance at the snow peaks and
glacier fields that are the Switzerland of the tourist. If he deals with the grand
catastrophes of nature, with avalanche, flood, and storm, it is in their relation
to the victims of the elements, for his topics are the people and their institutions.
We cannot entirely to the parable of his preface."—*Times.*

"A lively, interesting, and altogether novel book on Switzerland. It is full of
valuable information on social, political and ecclesiastical questions, and, like all
Mr. Dixon's books, it is eminently readable."—*Daily News.*

"We advise every one who cares for good literature to get a copy of this brilliant,
novel, and abundantly instructive account of the Switzers. The composition of the
book is in the very best style."—*Morning Post.*

"A work of real and abiding value. Mr. Dixon has never painted with more
force and truth. His descriptions are accurate, impartial, and clear. We most
cordially recommend the book."—*Standard.*

"A most interesting and useful work, especially well timed when the questions
of military organisation and primary education occupy so large a share of public
attention. There is that happy fusion of the picturesque and the practical in Mr.
Dixon's works which gives especially to the present book its great charm. It has
at once the graphic interest of a romance, and the sterling value of an educational
essay."—*Daily Telegraph.*

"Mr. Dixon has succeeded in giving the public a very inviting book. The reader
rises from it with the pleasant consciousness of having acquired useful information
without fatigue, and of having been as much interested by solid truth as if it were
fiction meant only to amuse."—*Echo.*

"Any respectable book on the Switzers and Switzerland is welcome to lovers of
the land and the people, and we trust that Mr. Dixon's volume will be read in Switzerland as well as in England."—*Athenæum.*

"Mr. Dixon's book contains much readable and instructive matter."—*Examiner.*

"A writer of much dramatic and descriptive power, and one who knows his way
to trustworthy sources of information, Mr. Dixon has given a clever and instructive
sketch of the salient features of the confederation. All who know the playground
of Europe will thank the writer for so clear an account of the social institutions of
a free people."—*Graphic.*

"This work is in every respect the most useful and the best by means of which
Mr. Dixon has introduced novel subjects all worthy of the utmost attention of his
countrymen, and illustrated them by so elegant a method of communication so im-
mensely to enhance their value."—*Messenger.*

"No such book has been written concerning Switzerland by any Englishman,
and few books of travel we possess unite more valuable information to more descriptive power and charm of style."—*Sunday Times.*

MESSRS. HURST AND BLACKETT'S
NEW WORKS—*Continued.*

A PERSONAL HISTORY OF THE HORSE
GUARDS, From 1750 to 1872. By J. H. Stocqueler. Author of
" The History of the British Army," &c. 1 vol. 8vo. 14s.

MODERN TURKEY. By J. Lewis Farley,
Consul of the Sublime Porte at Bristol. *Second Edition.* 1 vol. 14s.

Contents:—Beyrout; Belt-Miry; Mount Lebanon; Travelling in Syria and Palestine;
a Day with the Bedawins; Syria, Past and Present; the Empress Eugénie's
Visit to Constantinople; the Suez Canal; Turkish Women; Turkish Armaments; Public Instruction; the Capitulations; Turkey as a Field for Emi-
gration; British Interests in Turkey; Turkish Finances; the Stock Exchange;
Geographical Position of the Empire; Agricultural Products; Fisheries; Mines;
Petroleum; Roads; Railways; Docks and Harbours; Public Works, &c.

" Books on Turkey by impartial authorities are not very common, and we are
always glad to welcome anything that gives us the most recent information, and
appears to be written frankly and dispassionately."—*Times. Oct.* 12.

" ' Modern Turkey,' by J. L. Farley, is from a writer long familiar with the country,
and whose experience encourages a sanguine view of its future, alike as regards
social, political, and industrial advancement."—*Times: City Article. June 5.*

" Mr. Farley has a good deal of interesting information to communicate in regard
to the resources of modern Turkey; and we may add that he puts it briefly, clearly,
and in an agreeable style."—*Saturday Review.*

" Mr. Farley is to be praised for the admirable manner in which he has marshall-
ed his facts and arranged his matter. His style, too, is lucid and agreeable, and
he manages to clothe the dry skeleton of statistics with life and animation. His
book will do a great deal to remove many prejudices against Turkey from the
minds of Englishmen, and will bring very vividly before their eyes the present condition of a country about which great numbers of our countrymen are lamentably
ignorant."—*Examiner.*

" This very interesting and exceedingly well-written volume well deserves an
earnest perusal. It is a book of incalculable value."—*Messenger.*

" An able sketch of the present state and latest resources of the Ottoman Empire.
Mr. Farley writes ably and clearly, and few will put down his book without having
learned something new about the material resources of Turkey, and the aspirations
of its most enlightened statesmen."—*Graphic.*

" Mr. Farley evinces a thorough knowledge of his subject, and his work deserves
to be attentively perused by all who are interested politically, commercially, or
financially, in the Ottoman Empire."—*Liverpool Albion.*

HISTORY OF WILLIAM PENN, Founder of
Pennsylvania. By W. Hepworth Dixon. A New Library Edition.
1 vol. demy 8vo, with Portrait. 12s.

" Mr. Dixon's ' William Penn' is, perhaps, the best of his books. He has now revised and issued it with the addition of much fresh matter. It is now offered in a
sumptuous volume, matching with Mr. Dixon's recent books, to a new generation of
readers, who will thank Mr. Dixon for his interesting and instructive memoir of
one of the worthies of England."—*Examiner.*

" ' William Penn' is a fine and noble work. Eloquent, picturesque, and epigra-
matic in style, subtle and philosophical in insight, and moderate and accurate in
statement, it is a model of what a biography ought to be."—*Sunday Times.*

" The character of this great Christian Englishman, William Penn, a true hero
of moral and civil conquests, is one of the fairest in modern history, and may be
studied with profit by his countrymen of all ages. This biography of him now
finally put into shape as a standard work of its kind, is Mr. Dixon's most useful
production. Few books have a more genial and wholesome interest, or convey
more beneficial instruction."—*Illustrated News.*

" Like all Mr. Dixon's books this is written in a pleasing, popular style, and at the
present moment, when our relations with the United States are attracting so much
attention to the Great Republic of the new world, the re-appearance is most timely
and welcome."—*Erin.*

2

MESSRS. HURST AND BLACKETT'S
NEW WORKS—*Continued.*

THE LUSHAI EXPEDITION. 1871-72. By R.
G. WOODTHORPE, Lieut. Royal Engineers. 8vo, with Illustrations.
(In Dec.)

SPORT AT HOME AND ABROAD. By LORD
WILLIAM PITT LENNOX. 2 vols. crown 8vo. 21s.

"Two very amusing and instructive volumes, touching on all sorts of sport, from the experienced pen of a writer well qualified to handle the subject. Stored with interesting matter the book will take the fancy of all lovers of pastime by flood or field."—*Bell's Life.*

"This work is extremely interesting and instructive from the first page to the last. It contains a vast amount of useful information and excellent advice for the British sportsman, interspersed with an inexhaustible fund of anecdote."—*Court Journal.*

"Lovers of sport will welcome this new work by Lord W. Lennox eagerly. We have here experiences of sport of the most varied kind—from fishing in Upper Canada to fowling in Siberia; from Highland deer hunting to angling on the quiet banks of the Thames. Then descriptions of ancient and modern gymnastics, sports of England in the middle ages, hunting, fencing, wrestling, cricketing, and cockfighting. We may learn how to choose a yacht or a hound, a hunter or a rifle, from these useful and amusing pages, and there are also a great number of lively anecdotes to amuse the 'noble sportsman' when the fish won't rise, when the deer are shy, or the weather is unfavourable, or there is a dead calm for the yacht. We predict a great success for this book."—*Era.*

PRAIRIE FARMS AND PRAIRIE FOLK. By
PARKER GILLMORE ("Ubique"), Author of "A Hunter's Adventures in the Great West," &c. 2 vols. with Illustrations. 21s.

"Mr. Gillmore has written a book which will make the English reader take a deep interest in Prairie Farms and Prairie Folk. His narrative of his sojourn, his description of the country, and of his neighbours, are all most readable. Mr. Gillmore's sporting feats are the themes of some of his best chapters."—*Daily News.*

"This work is the very best of its class that Mr. Parker Gillmore has yet written, not merely because of its lifelike descriptions of open-air life in the vast outlying districts of the American continent, but because it gives an amount of information of incalculable value to emigrants."—*Messenger.*

"For anecdote, descriptions, and all kinds of information relating to sport it would not be easy to name a more effective and readable writer than Parker Gillmore."—*Illustrated London News.*

"We heartily recommend this work. The attraction of the author's descriptions is very great. His style is graphic, and his records are always entertaining and remarkable."—*Sunday Times.*

QUEEN CHARLOTTE ISLANDS: A Narrative
of Discovery and Adventure in THE NORTH PACIFIC. By FRANCIS POOLE, C.E. Edited by JOHN W. LYNDON. 1 vol. 8vo, with Map and Illustrations. 15s.

"There can be no doubt about the spirit of enterprise and power of endurance with which Mr. Poole is gifted, and much of his book is very exciting reading. Nor are the parts of it which are the least novel the least interesting. The chapters descriptive of his journeys round America, and across the Isthmus, with his account of San Francisco and Victoria, will repay perusal."—*Pall Mall Gazette.*

"As a whole the book is interesting and instructive, and its author evidently a pleasant and a plucky fellow. We can confidently recommend the book to all who wish to form an idea of life and land in those countries in the present, and of their capacity in the future."—*Athenæum.*

"This very interesting narrative is excellent reading. Mr. Poole has added much that is valuable to the stock of general information."—*Daily News.*

"This extremely interesting work—well written and well edited—is full of novelty and curious facts. It is one among the most fresh and instructive volumes of travel and adventure which have been produced for a long time."—*Standard.*

4

MESSRS. HURST AND BLACKETT'S
NEW WORKS—*Continued.*

BRIDES AND BRIDALS. By J. C. JEAFFRESON,
B.A., Oxon, author of "A Book about the Clergy," &c. 2 vols. 8vo, 30s.

CONTENTS:—Antiquity of Matrimonial Customs, Marriage by Capture, Marriage by Purchase, The Church Porch, Espousals, Celebration of Marriage, Publication of Banns, Ancient Restraints on Freedom of Marriage, Pre-Contracts, Marriages in Strict Order and Marriages by License, The Wedding Ring, The Ring-finger, The Bridal Ring, Costumes of Brides, Bridesmaids, and Groomsmen, Wedding Cake, Wedding Presents, The Dinner and the Dance, Sports and Pastimes, Bridal Music, Wedding Sermons, Infantile Wedlock, Lucky Days and Lawful Hours, Parental Authority, Discipline of Wives, Laws and Novels, Sermons and Essays, Old Proverbs about Marriage and Women, Characteristics of Womankind in Old Time, The Spinsters of Past Times, Medical Women and White Slaves, Clerical Marriage, Lay-marriages during the Commonwealth, Taxes on Celibacy, Curious Marriages, Clandestine and Irregular Marriages, Prisons and Lawless Churches, Fleet Marriages, The Fleet Clergy, Lord Hardwick's Marriage Act, The Savoy Chapel, Gretna Green Matches, The Carrying away of Heiresses, The Royal Fleet Marriages, The Royal Marriage Act, Marriage with Deceased Wife's Sister, Honeymoon Trips and Cards, Samuel Johnson on Matrimony, Jeux d'Esprit against Wives, Dissolution of Partnership, &c.

"Two very interesting and clever volumes. Happy in his subjects, and happy in his treatment of them, Mr. Jeaffreson has here maintained his old reputation, and has produced a book about brides and bridals as attractive as either of his well-known books about doctors, lawyers, or the clergy."—*Notes and Queries.*

" While these delightful volumes are certain to command the attention of men of 'all sorts and conditions,' women will feel that the book especially concerns themselves. Having consulted hundreds of volumes and unpublished records of obsolete customs, Mr. Jeaffreson, interspersing legal information with quaint and amusing anecdotes, has produced a work which will be found a most useful book of reference by historians, artists, and all persons who desire to know how our forefathers lived. The chapters on 'The Discipline of Wives,' and 'Old Proverbs about Marriage and Women,' are extremely interesting."—*Morning Post.*

"A book whose theme is sure to attract many readers. 'Brides and Bridals' is a subject in which we have all taken some part, or hope to do so, either as principals or as accessories. Yet probably very few of us know what is the real meaning and origin of the numerous rites with which a wedding is solemnised. The history and interpretation of these are told in a most interesting manner by Mr. Jeaffreson. His work will make a valuable addition to that social history of England whereof his 'Books About' lawyers, doctors, and clergy form the earlier volumes. In this his last work Mr. Jeaffreson has been very careful so to write that no mother need shrink from placing it in the hands of her maiden daughters."—*John Bull.*

THE LITERARY LIFE OF THE REV. WILLIAM HARNESS, Vicar of All Saints, Knightsbridge, and Prebendary of St. Paul's. By the Rev. A. G. L'ESTRANGE. 8vo. 15s.

Among other celebrated persons of whom anecdotes and reminiscences will be found in this work are Lord Byron, Sheridan, Scott, Crabbe, Coleridge, Moore, Rogers, Charles Lamb, Sydney Smith, Talfourd, Theodore Hook, Dickens, Thackeray, Lockhart, Lady Byron, Miss Mitford, Miss Austen, Joanna Baillie, Mrs Siddons, Madame d'Arblay, &c.

"The book is a pleasant book, and will be found excellent reading. All those to whom the good name of Byron is dear, will read with an almost exquisite pleasure the testimony given by Harness. The fine qualities of this man are set forth, without any attempt to conceal his errors or his vices; as regards the latter, there is shown to have been gross exaggeration in the report of them."—*Athenæum.*

"This work will be read with much interest. The Rev. William Harness was the friend of Byron, and of almost every literary celebrity of his time. He liked to be about literary men, and they reciprocated that liking. Byron, Miss Mitford, the Kembles, Wordsworth, Southey, Coleridge, Lamb, Rogers, Sheridan, Theodore Hook, Henry Hope, were among his friends; and the consequence of this varied literary friendship is that his life, for richness in biographical details, is surpassed by no recent publication except Crabb Robinson's Diary."—*Echo.*

4

13, Great Marlborough Street.

MESSRS. HURST AND BLACKETT'S
NEW WORKS—*Continued.*

VOLS. I. & II. OF HER MAJESTY'S TOWER.
By W. HEPWORTH DIXON. DEDICATED BY EXPRESS PERMISSION TO THE QUEEN. *Sixth Edition.* 8vo. 30s.

CONTENTS:—The Pile—Inner Ward and Outer Ward—The Wharf—River Rights—The White Tower—Charles of Orleans—Uncle Gloucester—Prince Rules—Beauchamp Tower—The good Lord Cobham—King and Cardinal—The Pilgrimage of Grace—Madge Cheyne—Heirs to the Crown—The Nine Days' Queen—Dethroned—The Men of Kent—Courtney—No Cross no Crown—Cranmer, Latimer, Ridley—White Roses—Princess Margaret—Plot and Counterplot—Monsieur Charles—Bishop of Ross—Murder of Northumberland—Philip the Confessor—Mass in the Tower—Sir Walter Raleigh—The Arabella Plot—Raleigh's Walk—The Villain Waad—The Garden House—The Brick Tower—The Anglo-Spanish Plot—Factions at Court—Lord Grey of Wilton—Old English Catholics—The English Jesuits—White Webbs—The Priests' Plot—Wilton Court—Last of a Noble Line—Powder-Plot Room—Guy Fawkes—Origin of the Plot—Vinegar House—Conspiracy at Large—The Jesuit's Move—In London—November, 1605—Hunted Down—In the Tower—Search for Gunpowder—End of the English Jesuits—The Catholic Lords—Harry Percy—The Wizard Earl—A Real Arabella Plot—William Seymour—The Escape—Pursuit—Dead in the Tower—Lady Frances Howard—Robert Carr—Powder Poisoning.

FROM THE TIMES:—"All the civilised world—English, Continental, and American—takes an interest in the Tower of London. The Tower is the stage upon which has been enacted some of the grandest dramas and saddest tragedies in our national annals. It, in imagination, we take our stand on those time-worn walls, and let century after century fill past us, we shall see in dim succession the majority of the most famous men and lovely women of England in the olden time. We shall see them jesting, jousting, love-making, plotting, and then anon, perhaps, commending their souls to God in the presence of a hideous masked figure, bearing an axe in his hands. It is such pictures as these that Mr. Dixon, with considerable skill as an historical limner, has set before us in these volumes. Mr. Dixon dashes off the events of Tower history with great spirit. His descriptions are given with such terseness and vigour that we should spoil them by any attempt at condensation. As favourable examples of his narrative powers we may call attention to the story of the beautiful but unpopular Elinor, Queen of Henry III., and the description of Anne Boleyn's first and second arrivals at the Tower. Then we have the story of the bold Bishop of Durham, who escapes by the aid of a cord hidden in a wine-jar; and the tale of Maud Fitzwalter, imprisoned and murdered by the caitiff John. Passing onwards, we meet Charles of Orleans, the poetic French Prince, captured at Agincourt, and detained for five-and-twenty years a prisoner in the Tower. Next we encounter the baleful form of Richard of Gloucester, and are filled with indignation at the blackest of the black Tower deeds. As we draw nearer to modern times, we have the sorrowful story of the Nine Days' Queen, poor little Lady Jane Grey. The chapter entitled "No Cross, no Crown" is one of the most affecting in the book. A mature man can scarcely read it without feeling the tears ready to trickle from his eyes. No part of the first volume yields in interest to the chapters which are devoted to the story of Sir Walter Raleigh. The greater part of the second volume is occupied with the story of the Gunpowder Plot. The narrative is extremely interesting, and will repay perusal. Another most subtle possessed of a perennial interest, is the murder of Sir Thomas Overbury by Lord and Lady Somerset. Mr. Dixon tells the tale skilfully. In conclusion, we may congratulate the author on this work. Both volumes are decidedly attractive, and throw much light on our national history."

"From first to last this work overflows with new information and original thought, with poetry and picture. In these fascinating pages Mr. Dixon discharges alternately the functions of the historian, and the historic biographer, with the insight, art, humour and accurate knowledge which never fail him when he undertakes to illumine the darksome recesses of our national story."—*Morning Post.*

"We earnestly recommend this remarkable work to those in quest of amusement and instruction, at once solid and refined."—*Daily Telegraph.*

c

MESSRS. HURST AND BLACKETT'S
NEW WORKS—*Continued.*

VOLS. III. & IV. OF HER MAJESTY'S TOWER.
By W. HEPWORTH DIXON. DEDICATED BY EXPRESS PERMISSION TO THE QUEEN. Completing the Work. *Third Edition.* Demy 8vo. 30s.

CONTENTS:—A Favourite; A Favourite's Friend; The Countess of Suffolk; To the Tower; Lady Catherine Maznara; House of Villiers; Revolution; Fall of Lord Bacon; A Spanish Match; Spaniolizing; Henry De Vere; The Master of Holland; Sea Affairs; The Pirate War; Port and Court; A New Romance; Move and Counter-move; Pirate and Prison; In the Marshalsea; The Spanish Olive; Prison Opened; A Parliament; Digby, Earl of Bristol; Turn of Fortune; Eliot Eloquent; Felton's Knife; An Assassin; Nine Gentlemen in the Tower; A King's Revenge; Charles I.; Pillars of State and Church; End of Wentworth; Laud's Last Troubles; The Lieutenant's House; A Political Romance; Philosophy at Bay; Fate of an Idealist; Britannia; Killing not Murder; A Second Buckingham; Roger, Earl of Castlemaine; A Life of Plots; The Two Penns; A Quaker's Call; Colonel Blood; Crown Jewels, King and Colonel; Rye House Plot; Murder; A Patriot; The Good Old Cause; James, Duke of Monmouth; The Unjust Judge; The Scottish Lords; The Countess of Nithisdale; Escaped; Cause of the Pretender; Reformers and Reform, Reform Riots; Sir Francis Burdett; A Summons to the Tower; Arthur Thistlewood; A Cabinet Council; Cato Street; Perrolt; Last Prisoners in the Tower.

"Mr. Dixon's lively and accurate work."—*Times.*

"This book is thoroughly entertaining, well-written, and instructive."—*Examiner.*

"These volumes will place Mr. Dixon permanently on the roll of English authors who have rendered their country a service, by his putting on record a truthful and brilliant account of that most popular and instructive relic of antiquity. 'Her Majesty's Tower;' the annals of which, as related in these volumes, are by turns exciting and amusing, while they never fail to interest. Our ancient stronghold could have had no better historian than Mr. Dixon."—*Post.*

"By his merits of literary execution, his vivacious portraitures of historical figures, his masterly powers of narrative and description, and the force and graceful ease of his style, Mr. Dixon will keep his hold upon a multitude of readers."—*Illustrated News.*

"These volumes are two galleries of richly painted portraits of the noblest men and most brilliant women, besides others commemorated by English history. The grand old Royal Keep, palace and prison by turns, is revivified in these volumes, which close the narrative, extending from the era of Sir John Eliot, who saw Raleigh die in Palace Yard, to that of Thistlewood, the last prisoner immured in the Tower. Few works are given to us, in these days, so abundant in originality and research as Mr. Dixon's."—*Standard.*

"This intensely interesting work will become as popular as any book Mr. Dixon has written."—*Messenger.*

"A work always eminently readable, often of fascinating interest."—*Echo.*

"The most brilliant and fascinating of Mr. Dixon's literary achievements."—*Sun.*

"Mr. Dixon has accomplished his task well. Few subjects of higher and more general interest than the Tower could have been found. Around the old pile clings all that is most romantic in our history. To have made himself the trusted and accepted historian of the Tower is a task on which a writer of highest reputation may well be proud. This Mr. Dixon has done. He has, moreover, adapted his work to all classes. To the historical student it presents the result of long and successful research in sources undiscovered till now; to the artist it gives the most glowing picture yet, perhaps, produced of the more exciting scenes of national history; to the general reader it offers fact with all the graces of fiction. Mr. Dixon's book is admirable alike for the general view of history it presents, and for the beauty and value of its single pictures."—*Sunday Times.*

7

MESSRS. HURST AND BLACKETT'S
NEW WORKS—*Continued.*

FREE RUSSIA. By W. HEPWORTH DIXON. *Third Edition.* 2 vols. 8vo. with Coloured Illustrations. 30s.

"Mr. Dixon's book will be certain not only to interest but to please its readers and it deserves to do so. It contains a great deal that is worthy of attention, and is likely to produce a very useful effect. The ignorance of the English people with respect to Russia has long been so dense that we cannot avoid being grateful to a writer who has taken the trouble to make personal acquaintance with that seldom-visited land, and to bring before the eyes of his countrymen a picture of its scenery and its people, which is so novel and interesting that it can scarcely fail to arrest their attention."—*Saturday Review.*

"Mr. Dixon has invented a good title for his volumes on Russia. The chapter on Lomonosoff, the peasant poet, is one of the best in the book, and the chapter on Kief is equally good. The descriptions of the peasant villages, and of the habits and manners of the peasantry, are very good; in fact, the descriptions are excellent throughout the work."—*Times.*

"We claim for Mr. Dixon the merit of having treated his subject in a frank and original manner. He has done his best to see with his own eyes the vast country which he describes, and he has visited some parts of the land with which few even among its natives are familiar, and he has had the advantage of being brought into personal contact with a number of those Russians whose opinions are of most weight. The consequence is, that he has been able to lay before general readers such a picture of Russia and the Russian people as cannot fail to interest them."—*Athenæum.*

TURKISH HAREMS & CIRCASSIAN HOMES. By Mrs. HARVEY, of Ickwell Bury. 8vo. *Second Edition.* 15s.

"Mrs. Harvey's book could scarcely fail to be pleasant, for the excursion of which it gives us an account must have been one of the most delightful and romantic voyages that ever was made. Mrs. Harvey not only saw a great deal, but saw all that she did see to the best advantage. She was admitted into Turkish interiors which are rarely penetrated, and, protected by an escort, was able to ride far into the mountains of Circassia, whose lovely defiles are full of dangers which seal them to ordinary travellers. We cannot call to mind any account written of late years which is so full of valuable information upon Turkish household life. In noticing the intrinsic interest of Mrs. Harvey's book, we must not forget to say a word for her ability as a writer."—*Times.*

ANNALS OF OXFORD. By J. C. JEAFFRESON, B.A., Oxon. Author of "A Book About the Clergy," &c. *Second Edition.* 2 vols. 8vo. 30s.

"The pleasantest and most informing book about Oxford that has ever been written. Whilst these volumes will be eagerly perused by the sons of Alma Mater, they will be read with scarcely less interest by the general reader."—*Press.*

"Those who turn to Mr. Jeaffreson's highly interesting work for solid information or for amusement, will not be disappointed. Rich in research and full of antiquarian interest, these volumes abound in keen humour and well-bred wit. A scholar-like fancy brightens every page. Mr. Jeaffreson is a very model of a cicerone; full of information, full of knowledge. The work well deserves to be read, and merits a permanent niche in the library."—*The Graphic.*

"These interesting volumes should be read not only by Oxonians, but by all students of English history."—*John Bull.*

A BOOK ABOUT THE CLERGY. By J. C. JEAFFRESON, B.A., Oxon, author of "A Book about Lawyers," "A Book about Doctors," &c. *Second Edition.* 2 vols 8vo. 30s.

"This is a book of sterling excellence, in which all—laity as well as clergy—will find entertainment and instruction: a book to be bought and placed permanently in our libraries. It is written in a terse and lively style throughout, it is eminently fair and candid, and is full of interesting information on almost every topic that serves to illustrate the history of the English clergy."—*Times.*

MESSRS. HURST AND BLACKETT'S
NEW WORKS—*Continued.*

LIFE AND LETTERS OF WILLIAM BEWICK,
THE ARTIST. Edited by THOMAS LANDSEER, A.R.A. 2 vols. large post 8vo, with Portrait. 24s.

"The interest for general readers of this 'Life and Letters' is derived almost entirely from anecdotes of men of mark with whom the artist associated, and of which it contains a very large and amusing store. His fellow pupil and old friend, Mr. Thomas Landseer, the famous engraver, has put the materials before us together with much skill and a great deal of genial tact. The literary sketches which Bewick made of Hazlitt, Haydon, Shelley, Keats, Scott, Hogg, Jeffrey, Maturin, and others, are extremely bright, apt, and clear."—*Athenæum.*

MY EXPERIENCES OF THE WAR BETWEEN
FRANCE AND GERMANY. By ARCHIBALD FORBES. 2 vols. 8vo.

SPIRITUAL WIVES. By W. HEPWORTH DIXON.
FOURTH EDITION. 2 vols. 8vo. With Portrait of the Author. 30s.

"Mr. Dixon has treated his subject in a philosophical spirit, and in his usual graphic manner. There is, to our thinking, more pernicious doctrine in one chapter of scores of the sensational novels which find admirers in drawing-rooms and eulogists in the press than in the whole of Mr. Dixon's interesting work."—*Examiner.*

THE CITIES OF THE NATIONS FELL. By
the Rev. JOHN CUMMING, D.D. *Second Edition.* 1 vol. 6s.

"Dr. Cumming's book will be read by many with advantage."—*Graphic.*

"The work before us contains much historical information of interest and value. We award applause here, as we expounded in his treatise on The Seventh Vial, the skill and diligence of the author in the vast and careful selection of facts, both physical and moral, the interest of each when taken singly, and the striking picture of the whole when presented collectively to the view."—*Record.*

THE SEVENTH VIAL; OR, THE TIME OF
TROUBLE BEGUN, as shown in THE GREAT WAR, THE DETHRONEMENT OF THE POPE, and other Collateral Events. By the Rev. JOHN CUMMING, D.D., &c. *Third Edition.* 1 vol. 6s.

"Dr. Cumming is the popular exponent of a school of prophetic interpretation, and on this score has established a claim to attention. His book furnishes an instructive collection of the many strange portents of our day. Dr. Cumming takes his issue very fairly. He has a case, and the gravity of the subject must command the attention of readers."—*Press.*

TRAVELS OF A NATURALIST IN JAPAN
AND MANCHURIA. By ARTHUR ADAMS, F.L.S., Staff-Surgeon R.N. 1 vol. 8vo, with Illustrations.

MEMOIRS OF QUEEN HORTENSE, MOTHER
OF NAPOLEON III. Cheaper Edition, in 1 vol. 6s.

"A biography of the beautiful and unhappy Queen, more satisfactory than any we have yet met with."—*Daily News.*

THE LADYE SHAKERLEY; being the Record of
the Life of a Good and Noble Woman. A Cheshire Story. By ONE of the HOUSE of EGERTON. *Second Edition.* 1 vol. 6s.

"This charming novelette pleasantly reminds one of the well-known series of stories by the author of 'Mary Powell.' The characters bear the same impress of truthfulness, and the reader is made to feel equally at home among scenes sketched with a ready hand. The author writes gracefully, and has the faculty of placing before others the pictures her own imagination has called up."—*Pall Mall Gazette.*

HURST & BLACKETT'S STANDARD LIBRARY

(CONTINUED.)

VIII.—CARDINAL WISEMAN'S RECOLLECTIONS OF THE LAST FOUR POPES.

" A picturesque book on Rome and its ecclesiastical sovereigns, by an eloquent Roman Catholic. Cardinal Wiseman has treated a special subject with so much geniality, that his recollections will excite no ill-feeling in those who are most conscientiously opposed to every idea of human infallibility represented in Papal domination."—*Athenæum.*

IX.—A LIFE FOR A LIFE.

BY THE AUTHOR OF " JOHN HALIFAX, GENTLEMAN."

" In ' A Life for a Life ' the author is fortunate in a good subject, and has produced a work of strong effect."—*Athenæum.*

X.—THE OLD COURT SUBURB. By LEIGH HUNT.

" A delightful book, that will be welcome to all readers, and most welcome to those who have a love for the best kinds of reading."—*Examiner.*
" A more agreeable and entertaining book has not been published since Boswell produced his reminiscences of Johnson."—*Observer.*

XI.—MARGARET AND HER BRIDESMAIDS

" We recommend all who are in search of a fascinating novel to read this work for themselves. They will find it well worth their while. There are a freshness and originality about it quite charming."—*Athenæum.*

XII.—THE OLD JUDGE. By SAM SLICK.

" The publications included in this Library have all been of good quality; many give information while they entertain, and of that class the book before us is a specimen. The manner in which the Cheap Editions forming the series is produced, deserves especial mention. The paper and print are unexceptionable; there is a steel engraving in each volume, and the outsides of them will satisfy the purchaser who likes to see books in handsome uniform."—*Examiner.*

XIII.—DARIEN. By ELIOT WARBURTON.

" This last production of the author of ' The Crescent and the Cross ' has the same elements of a very wide popularity. It will please its thousands."—*Globe.*

XIV.—FAMILY ROMANCE; OR, DOMESTIC ANNALS OF THE ARISTOCRACY.

BY SIR BERNARD BURKE, ULSTER KING OF ARMS.

" It were impossible to praise too highly this most interesting book. It ought to be found on every drawing-room table."—*Standard.*

XV.—THE LAIRD OF NORLAW. By MRS. OLIPHANT.

" The ' Laird of Norlaw ' fully sustains the author's high reputation."—*Sunday Times.*

XVI.—THE ENGLISHWOMAN IN ITALY.

" We can praise Mrs. Gretton's book as interesting, unexaggerated, and full of opportune instruction."—*Times.*

XVII.—NOTHING NEW.

BY THE AUTHOR OF " JOHN HALIFAX, GENTLEMAN."

" ' Nothing New ' displays all those superior merits which have made ' John Halifax ' one of the most popular works of the day."—*Post.*

XVIII.—FREER'S LIFE OF JEANNE D'ALBRET.

" Nothing can be more interesting than Miss Freer's story of the life of Jeanne D'Albret, and the narrative is as trustworthy as it is attractive."—*Post.*

XIX.—THE VALLEY OF A HUNDRED FIRES.

BY THE AUTHOR OF " MARGARET AND HER BRIDESMAIDS."

" If asked to classify this work, we should give it a place between ' John Halifax ' and ' The Caxtons.' "—*Standard.*

www.ingramcontent.com/pod-product-compliance
Lightning Source LLC
Chambersburg PA
CBHW020509270326
41926CB00008B/807